Strategies for World Class Products

The Design Council

The Design Council is recognized by the Government as the UK's national authority on design. The Council's main activities are the commissioning of research projects on design-related topics, particularly stressing design effectiveness to improve competitiveness, communicating key design effectiveness messages to target audiences and developing the Education and Training Foundation, which has a broad remit covering all aspects of design education and design in education.

The Design Council is also launching a new copublishing programme with Gower in the allied fields of design management and product development. This is one of the first books in the programme. A complete list of new titles is available from Gower Publishing, telephone 01252 331551.

Strategies for
World Class Products

Mike Farish

The Design Council

Gower

Published by
Gower Publishing Limited
Gower House
Croft Road
Aldershot
Hampshire GU11 3HR
England

Gower
Old Post Road
Brookfield
Vermont 05036
USA

Mike Farish has asserted his right under the Copyright, Designs and Patents Act 1988 to be identified as the author of this work.

British Library Cataloguing in Publication Data
Farish, Mike
   Strategies for World-class Products
   I. Title
   658.57

ISBN 0-566-07535-0

Lirary of Congress Cataloging-in-Publication Data
Farish, Mike.
   Strategies for world-class products/Mike Farish.
      p.   cm.
   Includes index.
   ISBN 0-566-07535-0
   1. Consumer satisfaction. 2. Quality assurance–Management.
   3. Quality of products. 4. Product management. I. Title.
   HF5415.5.F37 1995
   658.5'62–dc20   95-1550
                                                                      CIP

Designed and typeset in Great Britain by Mick Keates and Concise Artisans and printed in Great Britain by the University Press, Cambridge.

Contents

Acknowledgements

I am very grateful for the support and cooperation of all the companies featured in this book; without their help it would not have been possible to write it.

I would also like to thank the following for their contributions and helpful comments: Don Reinertsen, David Robson of Scottish Design, the staff of the Design Council who helped me to carry out research, and my patient editor, Suzie Duke.

1 Introduction

Successful manufacturing companies, whatever their size and market, have shown that strong performance depends on a fast response to rapidly changing customer demands. The advantage invariably goes to the company that can deliver improved products and services before its rivals. All companies must therefore anticipate and satisfy customers' expectations, and this means accessing and interpreting accurate market information and, through the use of modern design and development techniques, converting that information into products that people want. 'Good design' does not mean developing a product that is only innovative or attractive; it means developing one that not only has both those qualities but is also the right product for the market, is ergonomically and functionally sound and can be manufactured at an appropriate price without difficulty. It means designing products in a way which eliminates problems early in the process and prevents costly and time-wasting changes near or even after launch.

Achieving all this depends not only on input from skilled designers and engineers, but also on a well-managed design and development process which can benefit fully from the contributions of a wide range of disciplines. This book focuses on key ways in which companies can improve their design and development process and in so doing improve their products and financial performance. It presents a varied selection of case studies which demonstrate how improvements can be achieved and how establishing an integrated product design and manufacturing strategy is the key to long-term business survival.

Design and investment

Design is an investment, and the profile of design in a company should reflect this. Investing in R&D and in design skills, and supporting the investment with a well-managed product development process, brings long-lasting and sometimes dramatic benefits. The case studies in this book bear witness to this:

- improvements at Bonas Machine Company (Chapter 3) have brought the company a sixfold increase in turnover from £7 to £43 million;
- Soundcraft (Chapter 3) has built up turnover in one sector from zero to 30 per cent of its total £23 million;
- Boss (Chapter 4) has increased its turnover by 25 per cent;
- for one product range Marconi Instruments (Chapter 5) has halved product development timescales and doubled turnover;
- Weir Pumps' lean management approach (Chapter 5) has enabled it to weather the recession well and reduce costs and timescales on a continuous basis;
- Shandon Scientific's reorganization and redefinition of product development policy (Chapter 7) has achieved a 14 per cent higher return on sales.

Companies must invest effectively in new product development to be able to design and manufacture high added value products. Crosfield Electronics (Chapter 7) can attribute some of its success to the fact that it ploughs back about 10 per cent of turnover into R&D, but, aware that innovation alone was not enough, redefined its product development and manufacturing methodology. Investment and innovation are now supported by a carefully remodelled approach which has brought a wide range of benefits.

The design stage of development establishes the product (technology, quality, reliability and cost) and determines the manufacturing resources required by it. Design absorbs under 15 per cent of the costs of a new product but commits about 85 per cent: it creates the 'architecture' of the production activity. The design phase determines both direct and variable overhead costs and in the long term also the fixed costs. The source of productivity improvements therefore lies in the product's design, which largely dictates the nature of the manufacturing process and the financial structure of the company as a whole. Design, therefore, cannot be viewed as an activity segregated from any other stage of the whole product development lifecycle. It affects costs right through the cycle and must therefore be integrated into a well-managed process within which the financial and other repercussions of design decisions are carefully understood and monitored.

The role of senior management

For these reasons senior management must be involved in product design and development and take responsibility for it, making a conscious commitment to the goal of producing a steady flow of products which people really want to buy and use. This does not mean that the autonomy of product development teams should be restricted and their performance weakened; it means that product development strategy should be seen as a board-level responsibility and new development projects should be assessed and approved by senior management. For example at Weir Pumps the product development executive, consisting of senior sales and technical managers, reviews market developments, defines appropriate responses and monitors progress of current projects under the chairmanship of the managing director.

It is also the responsibility of senior management to ensure that the culture and structure of the organization empower teams to operate effectively and yet also allow regular monitoring to take place, as well as free exchange of ideas, easy communication and maximum exploitation of ideas and skills in the best possible sense. Functional, hierarchical structures should not be allowed to undermine lateral teamworking, without which design and development cannot proceed satisfactorily.

Effective design and development policies combined with the dedicated commitment of management to succeeding in today's difficult and demanding market conditions are the foundations on which manufacturing survival can be built. It is essential for senior management to understand that 'design' means converting 'live' market and user information into highly competitive, innovative, added value products that people aspire to buy. Change is never easy to implement, but the companies featured in this book exemplify the different ways in which a new approach to design and development *can* be implemented and the business benefits that can result.

2 The top priorities

- The key objectives ■ Focusing on customer needs
- Teamworking ■ Developing the right culture
- Computer support ■ Making change happen

As the previous chapter has pointed out, to survive in the long term, companies need to invest properly in design, manage design effectively and ensure that it is a fully integrated element of modern, streamlined product development. Today any senior manager wanting to improve his or her company's performance is faced with what must often be a bewildering barrage of acronyms, buzzwords and hyped techniques which claim to offer the key to success. The difficulty is knowing what is right for your company and how your company's competences, markets, size, resources and objectives relate to the idealistic methods that are recommended.

This book does not attempt to introduce new buzzwords or techniques, nor will it imply that improving performance and processes is easy. But it will emphasize that by targeting four key objectives and trying to achieve them in a way which best suits your company – rather than expecting one technique or technology to solve everything – performance and process improvements can be made. If the steps towards change are based on a thorough and realistic understanding of what your company can or cannot, and should or should not, achieve, changes will often be much less difficult to implement.

The key objectives

To improve product development, companies must concentrate on four key objectives, the routes to which may vary from one company to another. They must:

- focus on customer needs and make products that people want;
- encourage and motivate staff to work together well in teams with the same goal of producing the best possible product;
- bring about and maintain a company culture which makes this possible and makes full use of all the skills and ideas that people have to offer;
- introduce technology and systems which support these three overriding objectives.

Each chapter of this book concentrates on how achieving one of these four aims can solve the key product development problems which so many companies understandably experience:

- developing products which people do not want;
- launching products too late and spending too much time on the wrong parts of the process;
- making changes too late in the process;
- allowing development costs to escalate.

If the whole company is working together towards the single aim of producing better, quality products, it will become easier to conquer the key problems of time and cost. In an increasingly competitive global market, schedules are becoming shorter and shorter and in many cases products that are not launched on time will never reach the right profit levels. But each company must know, for each product, what the implications are of spending more time on a particular stage of the product development process. Often more time should be spent at the early stages of product development with the result that less time is spent at the end, but there will be occasions, depending on product and market, when longer development times are essential and rising costs can be justified. Each company must calculate its own equation.

Focusing on customer needs

A manufacturing company which does not focus fully on its customers and their conscious – or sometimes unconscious – requirements might as well work blindfold. Every aspect of company activity should be guided by this and should follow the key principles of:

- understanding the target market and aiming new products at niche markets where necessary;
- anticipating trends caused by factors such as demography, buoyancy of the economy, legislation, lifestyle and fashion;
- involving engineers and technologists in understanding the market, the customer and how products are used;
- collecting and analysing feedback from customers and taking action on it;
- developing detailed market, specification and performance targets for a new product before starting on design and prototyping activities;
- designing new products with modular elements or system features which allow the sharing of elements between different product ranges;
- developing incrementally improved products, which involve less cost, time and risk than totally new ones;
- developing products which are not only easy to use and maintain, but also attractive, safe functionally and environmentally, and reliable;
- aiming for the ideal of introducing products which have no real competitors in the marketplace.

The success of Boss, which designs and manufactures contract seating (see Chapter 4), is due to a determination both to satisfy customer needs and to maintain excellent relations with suppliers. This enables it to explore new technical possibilities that other companies shy away from and to live up to a reputation for speed and responsiveness amongst a prestigious list of 'blue chip' companies. (Boss Design)

The word 'customer' should be taken in the broadest sense to include suppliers, retailers, distributors and sub-contractors. Building strong, communicative relationships with each of these groups can be a great asset.

Teamworking

In today's increasingly competitive business world it is the companies who can ensure that their staff work well together making full use of their skills, ideas and experience that have the strongest advantage and are most likely to survive. Teamworking in product development means building the right teams for the type of product, competences and resources available. Teams can include not only representatives from all departments, but also sub-contractors, suppliers, representatives of retailers and distributors and also customers and users or other experts, who can all contribute to ensuring that the right product design is manufactured.

As is explained in Chapter 4, the basic principles of teamworking will need to be adapted according to the number and type of staff in your company. The experience of Acco-Rexel, for example (Chapter 7), demonstrates how this can work and how products are improved as a result. The product development process needs to be well understood so that bottlenecks, perhaps caused by scarce availability of particular skills, can be identified and prevented in the future.

Developing the right culture

Developing the right culture and management structure is essential in ensuring that people have the freedom and motivation to work well together in teams focusing on customer needs. Most of the case studies in this book feature companies who have succeeded in introducing and maintaining an informal culture in which people communicate and exchange ideas freely, at the same time as making sure that rigorous monitoring and reporting procedures are in place, and keeping senior management in touch with progress. A move away from autocratic, hierarchical management is essential and training and support for staff must be provided if changes are to be implemented successfully. It is up to senior management to give staff the chance to discuss changes before they happen and to give them a role in implementation, so that they will not have the feeling that what is happening is out of their control.

Computer support

New computer technology supports the three key objectives of focusing on the customer, teamworking and developing the right culture. It cannot itself achieve changes unless introduced and operating within a management structure which is already satisfactory. If the latter is not the case the introduction of new technology can make matters worse and often accentuate previously suppressed problems. Introduced at the right stage and into the right structure, IT can greatly improve performance, communication and the accessibility of information. In doing so it can facilitate teamworking and move the company on to new ways of working and new cultural attitudes.

Making change happen

Chapter 7 looks more closely at how companies set change in motion and how even when difficulties are encountered first time round this can itself be a valuable learning process: in the end it leads to improved performance and objectives being achieved with better understanding of management and process issues.

Change will be possible only if there is a clear understanding and tracking of the existing product development process and if any new process is widely understood, accepted and followed throughout the company.

The lean, customer-led company that gives its people the freedom and encouragement to perform within the right management structure will be a survivor in the marketplace. The design and development of a product should galvanize and harmonize every aspect of company activity and no aspect of design and development should be seen as an isolated process or be allowed to operate as such.

3 Focusing on customer needs

■ Defining the real requirements ■ Getting close to customers ■ Information sources ■ The importance of specifications ■ Case study – Renold Gears ■ Case study – Bonas Machine Company ■ Case study – Soundcraft Electronics ■ Key action points

The ultimate test of any product development project is that the products that result from it satisfy a market requirement. Sometimes products, most obviously in the fashion world, may create their own demand. The fact that a style, cut or colour of an item of clothing originates from a particularly well-known 'name' or follows a particularly popular trend may be enough to make it desirable to large numbers of people.

A similar phenomenon may occur in the world of product design, though again the product is likely to have overtones of fashionability. An obvious example is the ubiquitous personal stereo, of which the original and best-known example is the Sony Walkman. The product itself is in no way technically innovatory. It is simply a tape recorder that does not record. Nevertheless, the concept of the personal stereo is obviously sympathetic to a number of current, if rather generalized, trends in society. It makes music available in any location, much as the transistor radio did a generation previously. It also acts to some extent as a fashion accessory, a piece of high-tech jewellery. When it first appeared it was, moreover, something of a status symbol, much as the mobile telephone has become more recently. But it would be difficult to argue that the product satisfied either an explicit or clear market requirement of the sort that could have been identified by formal or informal market research techniques. Rather it was the result of an intuitive inspiration, though one that originated very significantly from a company renowned for possessing a 'product-oriented' internal culture and whose chairman has a much-reported habit of carrying the company's latest products around with him almost wherever he goes.

In most cases, however, successful products are those that are developed with the deliberate aim of satisfying specific, identifiable and well-researched market requirements – and those which, once market needs are identified, can be recognized as fitting into a coherent product strategy based on realistic understanding of a company's core competences and long-term objectives. Developing products that do satisfy identifiable market requirements is not a matter of chance or coincidence; it is achievable only by having in place the mechanisms which can ascertain real customer needs, transmit them back to the company and embody them in the specification for a new product development project. These mechanisms must also ensure that those clearly analysed and understood requirements remain the guiding principle for the work that ensues.

Defining the real requirements

There are numerous ways in which the goals of identifying and satisfying a market requirement can be achieved. Formal, questionnaire-based market research is one of the most obvious approaches and it remains a valuable tool. But one of the hallmarks of successful product design is increasingly the exploitation by companies of more innovative and imaginative ways of accessing market and user information. Perhaps the most direct means of interfacing market requirements with product development goals and processes is to provide development personnel with immediate experience of the end-user environment. This means letting engineering and other technical personnel – and also any other members of the product development team who need to – talk with customers and observe their activities first hand in order not merely to learn their requirements but also to understand the environment in which customers operate. The Honda example is often quoted. When Honda decided to develop new car models for the American market the company sent its team to the United States to live amongst the people who would drive them.

Getting close to customers

In other words, contact with customers should no longer be a segregated activity reserved for sales and marketing staff. Instead it should also become an everyday experience for many of the individuals with specialist design expertise who are directly involved in product development programmes. The approach is equally valid whether consumer or capital goods are involved. Whether the product is a chair, radio, a hair-dryer, specialist medical or testing equipment, or factory machinery, people have to use it. The way it is designed will affect their initial choice of model and whether ease of use and satisfactory performance encourage them to keep it or buy a new model from the same company.

Although involving design staff directly with customers is unlikely to be an inappropriate technique, many companies seem to be inhibited about employing it. Sometimes the reason may be a perception that the particular technical expertise

Design determines:

- performance
- quality
- reliability
- ease of use
- appearance for aesthetic and ergonomic reasons
- safety
- ease of maintenance, service and repair
- ease of disposal or recycling
- ease and speed of availability
- ease of manufacture

Industrial and engineering designers must all have firsthand acquaintance with what customers need, so that this awareness can feed into the factors that determine customer satisfaction.

involved is so specialized or complex that it cannot be effectively integrated with other activities. Generally, though, the reason is largely cultural – simply a feeling that dedicated design or engineering personnel are by their nature unsuitable company representatives. This attitude is often rooted in the mistaken, and outdated, belief that design is a discrete activity carried out in a segregated area by drawing office personnel. The issues of corporate culture and information management are discussed in Chapters 5 and 6, but for the moment it is worth recording that, whatever the volume or quality of market information flowing into a company, it will not guide the product development process unless there are both the structures to record, analyse and disseminate it and also a general ease of communication between people involved in the process.

Information sources

The immediate question is simple: how can a company find and utilize market information in ways which are more likely to give competitive advantage? This is not the same as simply asking what sort or amount of information may be available. A great amount may indeed be freely available – most obviously in the form of relevant business and technical publications, market analyses produced by third parties and competitor literature. All of this is potentially valuable and companies can make more or less use of it as necessary, but to gain competitive advantage companies need to exploit fully the data which is coming into the company

Analysing market information

Reasons for buying, by degree of importance		Customer satisfaction/dissatisfaction	
	Average importance (%)	Own company	Competitor
Reliability	20		
Price/value for money	18		
Delivery speed	15		
Product range	12		
Operating cost	10		
Design	7		
Performance	5		
Delivery reliability	4		
Features/options	4		
User-friendliness	3		
Other	2		

Information on customers must not only be collected and analysed but must also be accessible to those who need it. (Source: Arthur D Little Ltd)

all the time. They also need to go out proactively and talk to product users and experts in relevant fields to tap into previously unexplored sources. This means utilizing all in-house staff – not just specialist sales and marketing personnel but also senior management, design and production staff, and field maintenance and customer service employees. It means valuing and using the information available through sub-contractors, suppliers and consultants. Staff of sub-contracted firms must be regarded as immensely valuable and possibly unique sources of market information. The ways in which different types of information are gathered will vary depending on the source, the market and its size.

When assessing customer needs it is also important to distinguish to what extent their demands can be met, and as far as possible to what extent what people say they want will actually at a later stage – depending on the speed of product development – be substantiated in their purchases. It is pointless to produce what customers want now: companies must find a way of combining knowledge of what customers want in the present with speculation, tested as far as possible, about what they will want in the future. Information has to be correctly interpreted, although of course risks will always have to be taken.

The importance of specifications

One procedural principle of fundamental importance in focusing on customer needs is that of shaping all product development activities around a core specification document. The essential point about a specification is that it is not a determining factor in the product's final design in the conventional, limited sense of the word. In other words a specification does not necessarily stipulate a product's size, shape, colour or any other aspect of its geometry or appearance; it defines the expected performance characteristics and attributes of the end product and also the market constraints and targets of which it has to take account. Typical elements of a specification might, therefore, include:

- performance criteria of the 'how fast', 'how slow' category;
- target price;
- ergonomic needs;
- suitability for manufacture on particular production equipment;
- compliance with specific environmental or safety legislation;
- possession of specific attributes such as a minimum hardness or corrosion resistance;
- tolerance of particular external operating environments, for instance maximum and minimum temperatures;
- duration of operation between service and maintenance.

This does not mean, of course, that a specification might not make specific design requirements in terms, for instance, of appearance or materials to be employed. The specification for an executive chair, for instance, might stipulate that it must be leather-covered. But in general a specification must be framed as a set of targets that do not presuppose the means by which those targets are achieved.

The ensuing product development process must then be left free to find the best ways of achieving those targets – which ideally will not change once the specification has been agreed. But given that market conditions may change during the course of a product development project then the possibility of change in the specification itself must also be allowed for. Ultimately successful product development integrates adherence to a specification framed in terms of market and performance requirements with freedom for product development personnel to exercise the maximum degree of imagination and innovation in fulfilling those requirements.

The case studies which follow demonstrate how the principles described in this chapter can yield immense benefits and help companies to bring the right products to market.

Renold Gears' senior management, who have direct involvement in marketing activities, visit major agents and subsidiaries every year to gather market information. The company receives and analyses a constant flow of market data, and middle management ensure that product development is based from the start on real customer requirements. (Renold Gears)

Case study – Renold Gears

Based in Rochdale, Renold employs well over 400 people in the manufacture of geared motor units, speed reducers, clutches and couplings, all of which are supplied to other manufacturers for use in final applications as varied as machine tools and escalators. The company has an intense commitment to continuous new product development. The introduction of a dozen or so new or revised products over a two-year period is a typical achievement.

Renold has attained this level of activity by combining a proactive approach to marketing and a multidisciplinary management structure with a day-to-day product design operation that is of necessity highly specialized technically. It has, however, avoided making specialization an excuse for the segregation of product development operations and hence ultimately of their isolation from real market requirements. Instead, the direct involvement of senior management in marketing activities and the delegation of specific responsibility for monitoring market developments to selected middle management personnel ensure that product development projects are based from the start on an appreciation of real customer requirements.

The gathering of market information is an immediate responsibility of senior management. All the company's 17 sales subsidiaries worldwide are visited quarterly by either the managing director, sales and marketing director or export manager. At least another dozen major agents can expect such a visit each year. Significant clients at the major assembly companies receive similar treatment. Renold has also devolved to a designated individual within the sales department specific responsibility for investigating new product development projects being undertaken by clients and for involving the company in them. All of this means it receives a constant flow of market information that comes either directly from purchasers of the company's products or from intermediary sales agents. The information is immediate, up-to-date and highly relevant, and it provides data on real customers' immediate activities and future plans. It is not the sort of retrospective, aggregated information that a generalized, third-party survey of a particular industrial sector might generate.

What happens to customer information once it is inside the company is just as important. At Renold feedback is analysed in quarterly meetings involving all sales staff and both the sales and marketing director and managing director. Conclusions and recommendations from these meetings then become the raw material for a New Product Development Committee (NPD) which constitutes the core management structure in the company's product development process.

The composition of the NPD in itself underscores the importance the company attaches to the whole issue of product development. It comprises the managing director; the sales and marketing, technical, commercial and finance directors; the Design Office supervisor; and product managers from the company's manufacturing sites. The NPD's specific functions are to collate information from marketing analyses, prioritize the design department's workload, and monitor and evaluate feedback from product development programmes. The committee also decides on new product development projects and draws up the relevant technical and marketing briefs, which must be authorized personally by the managing director.

Renold has made the gathering and analysis of market information a top priority for senior management. It keeps in touch with client development activities; and it feeds customer information systematically into the product development process. For these reasons, and because the company fosters an unsegregated, multidisciplinary culture, guided by well-structured reviews, it can maintain a high output of quality products.

Case study – Bonas Machine Company

Another company for which the personal involvement of senior management in direct market research is a fundamental operational principle is Bonas Machine Company of Gateshead. Bonas employs about 400 people in the design and manufacture of electronic jacquards that are fitted to industrial weaving machines. By any standards the company is a success story. In the years from 1985 to 1994 turnover grew sixfold from £7 to £43 million, giving the company a near 50 per cent share of the worldwide market for electronic jacquard devices.

New product development at Bonas is a continuous activity and one in which the company has a proven track record of innovative success. In the middle 1980s it became the first company to introduce electronic jacquards, and subsequently pioneered the use of networked controllers permitting large numbers of weaving machines to be programmed simultaneously from a single point. But only a year before the introduction of the electronic jacquard the company was virtually bankrupt. Bonas admits now that lack of marketing and development of products without thinking through the implications of manufacturing, installation or servicing were the prime causes of its near demise.

A significant factor in Bonas' revival has been the manner in which it has approached the task of gathering basic customer information from an unusual, asymmetrical marketplace. The end users of the company's products are the members of a worldwide community of weaving firms. These are usually small- to medium-sized businesses with a high proportion of owner management. Personal contact at senior level is therefore the most effective marketing approach. An impersonal,

Bonas keeps in touch with all types of customers so that the product development team is fully aware of manufacturing, installation and servicing implications. The chairman and sales and engineering personnel are responsible for maintaining personal contact to monitor developments in the industry. (Bonas Machine Company)

questionnaire-based approach would, by contrast, run counter to the prevailing market culture.

The managing director of Bonas therefore spends a considerable amount of time acting as a travelling company representative liaising directly with counterparts in customer firms. But at the same time the company has to keep abreast of developments amongst the manufacturers of the weaving machines to which its own products are fitted. These weaving machine companies tend to be large, multinational corporations for which a more formal and structured marketing strategy must be implemented. This is accomplished by assigning individual sales and engineering personnel to the task of maintaining constant contact with specific machine-builders in order to monitor all relevant developments. In the final stages of any product development project both elements of this approach must be integrated, since both a weaving machine supplier and a weaving company must be persuaded to act as partners in the field-testing of new jacquard devices.

Bonas has won its new-found strength by looking more carefully at its market and working more closely with its customers. The implications of manufacturing, installation and servicing are now thought through and a more personal approach with potential and existing customers has brought tangible benefits.

Case study – Soundcraft Electronics

Ultimately all market feedback derives either from users or distributors. The approaches favoured by Renold and Bonas, whilst undeniably effective, are far from being the only available options. Indeed one of the hallmarks of successful and innovative product development is frequently the ability to display imagination and invention in the way market information is obtained in the first place. This may be especially necessary if the particular market sector involved exhibits any unusual characteristics. A company whose market and market response illustrate this point is Soundcraft Electronics of Potters Bar, Hertfordshire.

Soundcraft manufactures sound-mixing equipment for a broad range of customers that stretches from professional broadcasting and sound-recording studios to individuals involved in amateur and semi-professional music-making. That variety has immediate repercussions for both the company's new product development processes and associated market research activities. Despite the fact that the company is supplying products of basically similar functionality to all its customers – products aimed at amateur and semi-professional customers are to a large extent cut-down versions of those for the fully professional market – its overall market, viewed from a global perspective, is essentially a series of niches.

The company has in fact identified about 20 major market segments, each of which must be approached with products in which pricing and technical facilities are very finely tuned to suit a precisely defined set of requirements. Accordingly the company has ramped up its rate of new product development so that it now averages approximately one new product launch every month. Its success is evident from the fact that by 1993 some 30 per cent of its then £23 million turnover was generated by sales of products for the higher volume, lower price market with the generic brand name Spirit. Three years previously the proportion had been zero. Over the same period the company increased the number of products it offered by a factor of ten.

Soundcraft's strategy has been based on three key factors:
- a determination to gain a thorough understanding of the marketplace;
- the preparation of appropriately detailed new product specifications;
- and combining these priorities with a product development process in which small multidisciplinary teams provide an integrating mechanism within an informal company culture.

In the more specialist markets Soundcraft has always kept itself abreast of requirements by exploiting the fact that the market is a relatively compact 'global village' in which key individuals – for instance senior engineers and owners of equipment hire companies – can be easily identified. The company has endeavoured to liaise with these target individuals by various

Soundcraft's imaginative approach to users, who range from the high- to low-volume end of the market, has ensured competitive advantage. Events to which customers are invited help to stimulate exchange and discussion of ideas. (Soundcraft Electronics)

means such as inviting them to visit its factory, discussing their requirements and seeking their opinion on prototype products. In moving into the volume market Soundcraft has attempted to adapt the same approach to a broader audience. One entirely conventional means of doing so has been to build up a database of customer information through reply cards included with products sold. Another tactic has been to institute a series of 'live sound' seminars intended specifically for amateur and semi-professional customers. These are residential courses at which customers receive tuition in sound-mixing techniques from full-time professionals. At the same time Soundcraft's marketing and R&D staff are present to conduct informal market research through direct conversation with users of the company's products.

Such strategies are facilitated by the existence of key common features in different parts of the overall market. All products perform the same function, with differences deriving largely from the number and complexity of facilities. In addition 'aspirational feed-down' – the inevitable adoption at a lower price level of features first introduced in more expensive products – is a basic market characteristic.

Within Soundcraft the foundation for all new product development projects is a highly detailed specification document drawn up by the marketing department in cooperation with the relevant product manager. The document, which is of paramount importance, stipulates a target price for the product, as well as detailing technical performance objectives and functionality. Once a development project gets underway a small team is formed comprising one or more individuals from each of the R&D, production and test departments. The team leader may come from one of those areas, but may equally come from the marketing or sales departments.

Soundcraft has introduced imaginative and inventive methods to keep in touch with customer needs in contrasting markets. Although high- and low-volume requirements differ, ideas from each market cross-fertilize and ensure that products incorporate the features required at the appropriate price.

Key action points

Companies should aim to follow these principles to improve their market information and understand better what their customers need:

- Do not rely passively on market information which already exists. Make full use of your own company skills, experience and resources to investigate, record and analyse genuine customer needs; involve sub-contractors, suppliers, distributors and other specialists in the field.
- Do not impose on customers what you think they need but find out what they really need and why.
- Introduce design and development staff to actual customers and make sure they see for themselves how the product is perceived, used and criticized.
- Watch and even film your customers reacting to and using your products.
- In a sense your staff are customers too and all have ideas about the company's products: encourage and consider ideas from all sources.
- Make customers part of your team throughout the process right from the beginning.
- Make sure you are sufficiently aware of different needs for different markets and the different ways of gathering information from contrasting high- or low-volume markets: more personal contact for smaller markets, more computerized methods for larger.

■ Test products in every way possible with customers at every stage, through simulation, models and prototypes.

■ Differentiate between achievable and unrealistic customer requirements – some can be saved for the next product.

■ Set up activities and events to which you can invite customers, sub-contractors and suppliers to provide a forum for exchanging and developing ideas.

The degree to which marketing and sales personnel cooperate with more conventionally defined development staff during the product development phase is a fundamental influence on how much the product development process remains focused on defined market requirements. The next chapter explores the dynamics of teamworking during the product development phase from the definition of market requirements to product launch.

Teamworking

One of the most salient and consistent attributes of enlightened product design and development procedures is the adoption by companies of a teamworking approach. In its most thorough manifestations this technique means that complete responsibility for developing a specific new product is devolved to a multidisciplinary team with members drawn from both purely 'commercial' company departments, such as sales and marketing, and from design and engineering functions, including both traditionally defined front-end design operations and those concerned with manufacturing, quality control and even in-field servicing.

Concurrent Engineering

The fundamental ambition in teamworking is to achieve Concurrent Engineering (CE), which can be defined as ensuring that the various discrete activities involved in product development, for instance market research and at the other extreme prototype-testing, take place ideally as simultaneous operations or at least as an integrated sequence of events. The benefits should include both better products and drastically compressed development timescales.

Team composition

Teamworking can, however, take various forms. It is not a rigid methodology. Team members, for instance, may either be dedicated full time to the project concerned or they may retain other responsibilities elsewhere. There may be a mix of dedicated and part-time members. The team may contain representatives of all the skills required for the project or it may access certain resources maintained elsewhere on an as-needed basis. The most senior levels of management may take part in the team's activities on a day-to-day level or may maintain a watching brief from a distance – though not too great a distance.

All these factors and others depend upon size of company, corporate culture, the type of product and market, and availability of resources. These will obviously vary from one company to another, but certain conditions must always exist. Simply bringing an hitherto disparate group of individuals together will not necessarily make them into a team. In order to be effective, teams, both collectively and individually, need to be properly motivated and led. They are also likely to need appropriate education and training, and should have:

■ shared goals, values and understanding of the issues;
■ an understanding of how to add value for the customer;
■ clear, easy communication and quick, constructive decision-making powers;
■ defined roles, responsibilities, accountabilities and authority;
  ■ an understanding of the overall development process and

Team structures

Function/project relationship (F/P)	Form of teamwork	Characteristics
F1 Marketing P F2 Design F3 Manufacturing	'Over the wall'	• traditional functional empires - many changes and rework
P1 P2 P3	Dedicated project teams	• small teams of multiskilled people • a pool of staff or contractors pulled together for each project • similar repeat products/projects for different customers
P F → P1 P2 P3	Front-end design team Specifying projects that go through to manufacture	• clear design definition split into project or product modules for implementation • one project could represent a subcontractor or supplier
Fa → P1 P2 P3 Fb → Fc → F1 F2	Front-end multifunctional project team Frozen specification passed to function areas to progress	• functional split, ie electronic hardware, software, mechanical parts etc • needs very clear interface specifications and strong project management for handover
P1 P2 P3 F1 F2 F3	Matrix management Project team led through to completion Functional areas have technical responsibility	• functional contributions to project management and led through project team structures • used for projects requiring multiple functional inputs
P1 P2 P3 F1 F2 F3	Functional control Functional team members support several projects	• project manager responsible for achieving programme but team members retain functional reporting • use where specialists' functions have major input into a project
P1 P2 P3 F1 F2 F3	Coordination Functional area staff work in informal teams with other areas. Project targets and progress agreed jointly.	• small teams working in a collaborative and flexible environment

A key feature of enlightened product development procedures is teamworking, but the team structure will be determined by the type and size of company, the product and its market, and the resources available. (Barry Brooks, PA Consulting Group)

adverse financial and other effects of delays and late launches;
- an understanding of the value of CE and an ability to implement it;
- an ability to give priority to the project and corporate requirements rather than their own individual ambitions.

The issues of team size, membership and procedures have received a good deal of attention from various experts and analysts, and getting the size, character and membership of teams right can prove problematic. As has already been pointed out, there is in fact great variety in the composition of teams from one company to another, and there is often – and often needs to be – similar elasticity in the areas of full-time versus part-time membership and in how communications adapt. Research has shown that there tends to be more of a bias towards part-time team membership, although a major percentage of some industries, for example computer equipment manufacturers (nearly 90 per cent), use fully dedicated teams (EDS/Design Council 1994).

One of the most respected commentators on product

Guidelines for team staffing

1 Choose the team leader carefully.
2 Keep team size or sub-teams below ten members.
3 Use full-time team members only.
4 Use volunteers.
5 Disengage team members from other duties.
6 Locate team members together.
7 Assign members early and keep them together.
8 Use the best possible people.
9 Provide the team with all the required skills.
10 Use multi-skilled team members and generalists.

Team structure must be appropriate to project, timescales and resources. Don Reinertsen's research shows that these guidelines should be followed for rapid product development. (Source: Reinertsen Associates) development issues is the American, Don Reinertsen. His research on rapid product development has led him to formulate a set of 'rules' for team staffing, which taken together seem idealistic, but are worth bearing in mind as a benchmark against which companies can compare their own approach to teamworking and at least be forced to justify their disparities.

Not surprisingly, when teams are formed they universally contain one or more individuals who can be described as a design engineer, but across different industrial sectors there tend to be marked disparities in the relative frequencies with which individuals with other technical or commercial specialisms take part in team-based product development. In general most companies utilizing a team-based approach involve representatives of production engineering, sales and marketing, purchasing and supply, quality control and R&D. Mistakenly, rather less importance is attached to the inclusion of personnel from the maintenance, instrumentation and control, field service and legal departments, despite the important contribution which they can make.

Overall team autonomy is another area of contention.

The test of teamworking – does team or functional strength dominate?

1 Who approves change of the product specification?
2 Who can authorize a change of the selling price?
3 Who approves the assignment of individuals to teams?
4 Who makes trade-offs between key programme objectives?
5 Who can reassign people to work outside their speciality?
6 Who carries out performance evaluations affecting the promotion of individuals?
7 Where are organizations most important to career paths?
8 Which axis holds the best paid individuals?
9 Which axis is likely to win an argument?
10 Which axis controls the development budget?

Teams must have sufficient autonomy and must not be hampered by functional structures. (Source: Reinertsen Associates)

Common sense indicates that once a team has been formed the best policy is to endow it with maximum autonomy within the confines of an agreed reporting and monitoring structure. If a team is integrated too closely with an existing functionally-defined, departmental structure then its role and purpose often become diluted and the worth of its existence in the first place is questionable. There may be valid reasons why companies cannot implement completely autonomous, full-time teams. Scarcity of resources is the most obvious and in reality companies usually have to make compromises. Sometimes specific technical facilities and their associated personnel, for instance a CAD system or test laboratory, may need to be treated as a central resource to be accessed equally by various teams and even continuing departmental work. The choice of autonomy versus integration is also driven by the nature of the development programme. As Don Reinertsen comments: 'Team autonomy leads to faster decision-making, which is important when development speed is critical. However, when development objectives like low development cost or low product cost dominate, then tighter integration with existing departmental structures is usually necessary.'

In all types of teamworking regular and effective communication and the use of regular project review meetings are essential. Communication is improved if teams are co-located, in fact it is often the case that even the difference of a corridor between team members can have as dramatic a negative effect as sites a further distance away. (The computer equipment sector again leads the way with nearly 60 per cent of such manufacturers co-locating all team members.) Companies which do employ full-time team membership naturally perceive that individuals who are working with each other constantly can

NuAire recently remodelled its product development processes by introducing multifunctional teamworking involving commercial and technical disciplines right across the company. Integrated, multifunctional teams enjoy a large degree of autonomy. The company's DuctMaster range of fans was developed by an eight-strong team drawn from disciplines ranging across product development, manufacturing systems analysis and purchasing. (NuAire)

do so most effectively if they are situated right next to each other.

The next two case studies show how teamworking approaches can vary in different environments and different sectors.

Case study – NuAire

NuAire Limited of Caerphilly provides a clear example of teamworking in action.

The company employs 220 people in the design and manufacture of air-moving equipment for building ventilation purposes. It recently remodelled its product development processes by introducing multifunctional teamworking involving commercial and technical disciplines right across the company. The move followed on from a previous ineffective attempt to superimpose a multidisciplinary management review process onto a conventional departmental structure. Now a product review committee comprising board members and senior managers approves new development projects and reviews their progress every month. The day-to-day work, however, is carried out by integrated, multifunctional teams which enjoy a large degree of autonomy.

The company's DuctMaster range in the MasterClass family of axial flow fans was developed in this way. Responsibility lay with an eight-strong team drawn from disciplines ranging across product development, manufacturing systems analysis and purchasing. The team was encouraged to develop its own way of working and formulated a set of self-imposed rules to maximize its own efficiency, which included prohibiting arguments, avoidance of jargon and setting strict time limits on meeting durations. Each meeting concluded with the agreement of precise targets for the next working period. Manufacturing issues were considered at each stage of the project, which made the transition to production perceptibly smoother than in previous instances. Product support literature was written in a controlled and timely manner rather than hurriedly and belatedly.

Having adopted this new teamworking approach, the company found that it experienced 'spontaneous generation of ideas'. The simple fact that prototype models were analysed by the team as a group, rather than separately and singly as individuals, was a vital factor in promoting innovation at the design stage. The introduction of teamworking supported by training has enabled NuAire to focus resources more accurately and effectively and to develop products more quickly and efficiently.

Case study – Autohelm

Autohelm demonstrates how teamworking principles work in a different field.

Based in Portsmouth and now owned by the American Raytheon Corporation, Autohelm manufactures autopilots, navigation systems and instruments for the leisure marine market. The 200-strong company has an apparently conventional structure with rigid, vertical divisions by function into discrete departments such as sales and marketing, technical and production. But Autohelm makes broad-based ease of communication and access to business information basic operational principles. Against this background it implements a concise, highly focused approach to product development by which small core teams work within a well-defined framework of timetables, responsibilities and review procedures.

Immediate responsibility for specific projects at Autohelm rests with a core team of three personnel representing production and the key design disciplines of mechanical and electronic engineering. Around half the 30 design staff within the technical department are usually dedicated to a specific development team at any one time. Each team works to a detailed specification and timetable agreed by a multidisciplinary group of senior managers headed up by the managing director. The timetable takes the form of a simple checklist issued to each team at the start of a project. Crucially the timetable lays down immovable milestones in the form of management review meetings at key points such as the release of production tooling and completion of prototyping.

Each product development team has a 'champion', usually a

At Autohelm immediate responsibility for specific projects rests with a core team of three personnel representing production and the key design disciplines of mechanical and electronic engineering. Around half the 30 design staff within the technical department are usually dedicated to a specific development team at any one time. (Autohelm)

departmental manager, who acts both as an intermediary with other activities and as an arbiter of internal team disagreements. Teams call on extra resources within the company as they are required, but resource allocation is managed centrally to avert the possibility of confusion or clashes. Autohelm effectively combines the integration inherent in a team approach with the accountability and control provided by specific individuals retaining responsibility for key issues. A teamworking approach is also evident in the way Autohelm obtains and processes market research information (see page 73).

The importance of training

Autohelm's team champions act as a reminder that by itself the introduction of teamworking does not automatically generate positive results. Things can go wrong and will do so unless there are mechanisms for resolving conflicts and ensuring that all activities are focused on the fulfilment of defined objectives. Appropriate training beforehand, most obviously in teamworking skills such as communication, is also likely to be necessary. Whilst spontaneous generation of ideas may well be a benefit of teamworking, getting the team to function effectively in the first place is likely to require the implementation of specific enabling measures.

NuAire's teams operate in a 'training-rich' environment. The company operates a broad-based training programme intended both to foster an appropriate culture and impart specific skills. It defines its aim as being to make continuous improvement an integral part of its approach to product development. The company wants to make its personnel regard themselves not as technical specialists but as 'business people who also possess particular expertise'. All its product development team members have had specific training in teamworking. Interestingly, however, the company does not regard the provision of training itself as a particular expertise. It has no training department, but instead devolves responsibility for it to departmental managers, so training is an integrated – and integrating – company activity.

Bonas, featured in Chapter 3, also makes training an integral and continuous company activity, in which training for teamworking is regarded as an essential support for product development initiatives. The company in fact has a target of two weeks training per individual per year. There are two types that are particularly favoured by the company:

- Cross-discipline training in which individuals from different departments attend the same courses simultaneously is implemented as a deliberate policy. This is seen as a vital component of the general background support for team-based product development, particularly where the training involves techniques for continuous improvement and problem-solving.
- Outward bound courses are also used to build team spirit and attitudes favouring mutual support and cooperation.

A significant indicator of the importance Bonas attaches to training is that it has no pre-set training budget.

Monitoring and control

Successful teams are likely to exhibit a number of factors, which though they may seem trivial in some ways are in fact symptomatic of good practice. They will, for instance, have an agreed set of rules governing both collective and personal conduct. Typically their meetings will run to an agreed timetable and a pre-set duration. Nevertheless, informality and ease of communication should be the predominant procedural style.

This mix of apparently divergent elements is not necessarily contradictory as long as the correct overall controlling mechanisms are employed. Of these, regular reporting to senior management is, perhaps, the most important. A second is a requirement for fidelity to a previously agreed product specification document, which can only be altered through pre-set procedures involving senior management. A third is continuity of team membership. A fourth is a requirement for all team members to record an opinion and give their specific assent when collective decisions are made. This makes it impossible for an individual subsequently to disclaim responsibility for any decision supposedly made collectively by the whole team.

Case study – Amersham International

Amersham International is a company whose first foray into team-based product design was, in fact, their first venture in product design, conventionally defined, of any sort. Their experience shows how companies can work through initial difficulties to achieve a teamwork approach that will succeed even with geographically dispersed personnel and technical inexperience.

Amersham introduced the Hy-Lite™ hygiene monitoring system in late 1992 in response to critical new factors perceived to be affecting the food industry. Increasing consumer aversion to foods containing preservatives meant that manufacturers were having to implement proactive, preventive rather than retrospective, detective methods of ensuring the safety of food products, particularly for the accurate identification of sources of microbacterial contamination of manufactured foodstuffs. The problem was that existing methods of analysis required the use of loose chemicals by skilled personnel. They were therefore restricted to a laboratory environment and this imposed a delay between the gathering of samples and the generation of test results.

Amersham realized that there was an opportunity for a product that could be used by unskilled individuals in the field to produce similar results in real time. It therefore commissioned an external design consultancy to produce concept drawings for a 'pen', a syringe-like device that gathers a set volume of test material for sampling and then mixes it with reagents stored in the body of the pen in both liquid and freeze-dried forms. The consultancy also produced a similar outline for a luminometer to measure the extent of microbacterial material present by recording the amount of light given off by the resulting chemical reaction in the pen.

At this point overall responsibility for managing the development project was delegated in house to the company's technical director. The task was complex and demanding. The pen alone required the implementation of several technologies in which the company had minimal experience, including precision injection-moulding and foil-sealing for freeze-dried materials. In fact the company had no previous experience whatever in 'device development'. Its existing business comprised the packaged delivery of chemicals and radioactive materials.

Despite this, the company succeeded in developing an innovative product package by consciously adopting a development methodology based on multifunctional teamworking. At the same time Amersham used the key competences of its suppliers and maintained constant liaison with potential customers to ensure the product met defined market requirements.

Development of the pen was made the responsibility of a core project team with representatives from departments as diverse as manufacturing, quality control, marketing, instrumentation, legal, finance, purchasing and statistics. In their turn the team members, drawn from four different sites across the UK, coordinated the work of their own departments.

One task was to find a plastics moulding company not only capable of manufacturing the pen, but also willing to become a proactive contributor to the product development process. A suitable company was located in North London and

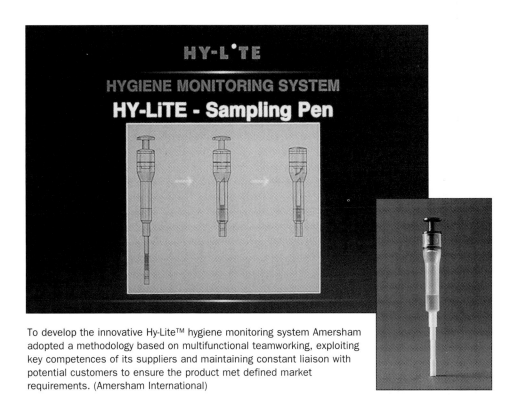

To develop the innovative Hy-Lite™ hygiene monitoring system Amersham adopted a methodology based on multifunctional teamworking, exploiting key competences of its suppliers and maintaining constant liaison with potential customers to ensure the product met defined market requirements. (Amersham International)

is now sole supplier of the pens to Amersham. Amersham's experience indicates that the essential elements of a supplier relationship, besides technical competence, are enthusiasm and trust. The company was selected in large part because of its general attitude and now works without a contract.

Within 12 months Amersham had finalized the configuration of the pen. It then tested market reaction in depth by sending development personnel out into the field to discuss its use with potential customers in around 20 target companies. Both scientific and marketing personnel were involved in this exercise, a clear breach of what would normally be regarded as functionally-defined responsibilities.

From its experience Amersham learned to overcome some of

the difficulties of product development, and succeeded in resolving those particularly related to an autonomous team-based approach. Responsibility for the luminometer was originally delegated to a team of external designers, plastics moulders and other manufacturers managed by a junior member of Amersham's own staff. Resulting problems required the appointment of a more senior individual. Nevertheless, the company brought an innovative, precisely-targeted product to the marketplace within a restricted timescale. It also managed to achieve this with geographically diffuse personnel, inexperienced in device development, and with much essential technical competence vested in scientific rather than engineering staff. Its success, however, derived from the adoption of an enlightened development methodology. The clear inference must be that there is nothing intrinsically difficult about adopting a team-based, market-oriented approach to product development.

Supplier relationships

'Teamwork' can and should involve suppliers and sub-contractors as well as employees. Building open, positive relationships with outside parties with whom you do business is a key to long-term survival and is fundamental to many companies' success. Suppliers and sub-contractors are also a valuable source of ideas and feedback on products, and relationships with them should ensure that they feel free to communicate useful information as well as reliably provide what they are contracted to provide.

Case study – Boss Design

Boss Design of Dudley in the West Midlands (see also page 8) is an example of how valuable good relationships with suppliers can be. The company designs and manufactures metal- and timber-framed contract seating such as managers' swivel chairs, armchairs and sofas for corporate reception areas, and stacking chairs for conference suites. Since its inception in 1983 it has developed steadily. It now employs 30 people and recent performance has brought an increase of 25 per cent on previous turnover.

The company has established a reputation for speed and responsiveness that has enabled it to build up a prestigious list of 'blue chip' clients. Recently it produced a prototype sofa for BT only 10 days after first sight of outline drawings.

The fact that 40 per cent of Boss Design's income is generated by bespoke contracts rather than by the sale of catalogue items indicates the importance to the company of completing projects rapidly and reliably.

A key element in its ability to do so is the way it interacts with its network of materials and component suppliers. Personal contact at a senior management level and an emphasis on quality rather than cost enable it to integrate the suppliers' own specialist expertise into highly compressed product development schedules.

In the case of the BT sofa, chief designer Hilary Birkbeck liaised directly with the fabricator of the wood frame and was therefore able to provide immediate approval and comments on the work. Hilary is in touch with the supplier twice a week as a matter of routine and the company's managing director, Brian Murray, maintains a similar close involvement with the supplier base.

The company has at least 30 active suppliers. Whilst it monitors prices and occasionally seeks secondary quotations, it is more concerned with ensuring the required levels of speed and quality through trust and direct communication. It therefore regularly seeks advice and comment on product development issues and rewards co-operative attitudes with repeat business. As a result it can obtain leather and fabrics overnight or foam within 48 hours and can be sure of receiving metal items within 20 days.

The way Boss Design manufactures chairs also illustrates the company's constant eagerness to explore new technical possibilities and contacts. The baseplate for each chair is cut by laser, an innovation for the company. The shock-absorbing spring is supplied by a company discovered by Hilary Birkbeck when he visited an exhibition devoted to railway industry requirements. A spring manufacturer, based in Sheffield, showed itself to be interested, co-operative and able to meet development timetables. It has therefore acted as supplier for important contracts. As a final touch prototypes are demonstrated to suppliers involved to let them see the finished product. 'To get the best out of suppliers' Hilary comments, 'products have to be sold to them as well as to clients'.

This innovative and exploratory approach to technical and commercial relationships in support of a reactive but flexible market profile is one of the company's essential characteristics. Hilary Birkbeck's philosophy is that 'you have to believe that someone, somewhere makes what you are looking for. The effort is in finding them!'

The way the company utilizes its supplier base is also an important factor in supporting its strategy for design protection. Whilst the company formally registers all its product designs, it also seeks to build in features that will make them difficult for competitors to replicate without incurring excessive costs or producing obviously inferior copies.

Boss Design illustrates that a positive, proactive attitude to suppliers and an outward-looking approach to product development is a highly effective lever for commercial success even in a relatively small company. Through commitment and communication Boss succeeds in competing effectively with much larger rivals in terms of quality and reliability, whilst simultaneously offering advantageous pricing structures.

Key action points

Before embarking on a new or more comprehensive team-based approach, look at how competitor companies structure and manage teams and how companies the same size as yours approach teamwork:

- Decide what sort of teamworking best suits your company and your business.
- Decide how to introduce the new approach: it may be best not to adopt it throughout the company to start with.
- Make sure you and your staff are clear about the benefits and that staff are fully supported with training.
- Think through how functional and team relationships will affect each other and how company culture should adapt to prevent problems of insecurity.
- Ensure that teams have clear objectives and focus fully on the right product for the customer.
- Ensure that multidisciplinary teams can function as they need to but that monitoring and review is well structured and responsibilities clear.

5 Developing the right culture

■ Cultural support ■ Case study – Marconi Instruments
■ Supporting the teamwork environment ■ Case study –
Weir Pumps ■ Case study – Maclaren ■ The key principles

In the broadest terms any company's product development
operations must ideally fit a layered structure of objectives.
Product development operations must in turn be supported by
the right culture and management attitudes.

Cultural support

While teamworking and the fusion of multidisciplinary
competences are essential to effective product development they
are by themselves only enabling methodologies. At a deeper level
something more is required: the orientation of the whole
company towards the goal of sustained, innovative product
development. Virtually every corporate activity has a part to play
and, accordingly, the streamlining, focusing and selection of
resources at the broadest level is necessary. To put it another way,
whilst the product development teams engaged for a finite
period on specific projects represent a discrete allocation of
resources aimed at the fulfilment of a specified goal, they should
also be a microcosm of the way the whole company operates on
a continuous basis.

Companies therefore need to understand not just their
markets but also themselves. They need to know their own
strengths and weaknesses so as to be able to marshal their own

resources effectively. They must ensure that the whole corporate structure is permeated by the right culture and attitudes, and supported by the broadest possible dissemination of relevant information as well as by appropriate skills and competences. Without this foundation of information, training, and supportive culture any of the best organizational procedures and techniques may come to grief.

One company that has built this essential foundation to its product development processes is Renold Gears, previously featured in Chapter 3. The company's great strength in product development terms is the way it meshes multidisciplinary marketing and management strategies with a core of highly specialized technological design expertise that must of necessity remain a discrete, stand-alone resource. The company has also realized that by themselves the right structures and procedures are not sufficient. People need to be confident about using them. It therefore ran a company-wide training programme in communication skills using an external consultant. All employees received some tuition against the background of their own responsibilities in a rolling two-year corporate plan.

As a result of this training programme the company reports that discussions are now much more sharply focused, dialogue is more open and fewer assumptions are made. The whole product development procedure, already closely managed and targeted, has become even more efficient.

Some specific examples illustrate the benefits which Renold has perceived:

■ The first models in its Ritepower range of gearboxes took only 12 months to develop, as opposed to the 3 to 5 years that might previously have been required. Of those 12 months no less than 5 were spent in the marketing phase.

- The subsequent rapid technical development of the product was made possible by its closely defined targets. One product needed to capture only 10 per cent of its total potential market to break even on its development costs.
- The involvement of manufacturing staff in development of this product meant that an initial projected requirement for a capital investment of £500,000 in new production equipment could be cut to £100,000.

Case study – Marconi Instruments

It is also enlightening to look at how another company manufacturing highly specialist equipment manages its product development processes, and encourages its staff to work in a more communicative, open culture.

Marconi Instruments, part of GEC, designs and manufactures test and measurement equipment for four distinct application areas – microwave, radiocommunications, telecommunications and printed circuit board manufacture. Each area makes its own technical and marketing demands, but also possesses some crossover in both customer identity and technological requirements.

The company has adopted a corporate structure which mirrors that of its marketplace. It has four Product Groups, accounting for around 200 personnel in total, each comprising a 'core' of sales, marketing and engineering specialists. Each group researches its own respective market sector, formulates product responses to perceived demands and leads the ensuing development programmes. But the company exercises centralized control over the allocation of development budgets and also maintains a common pool of technical expertise in areas such as generation of pcb artwork, systems engineering and

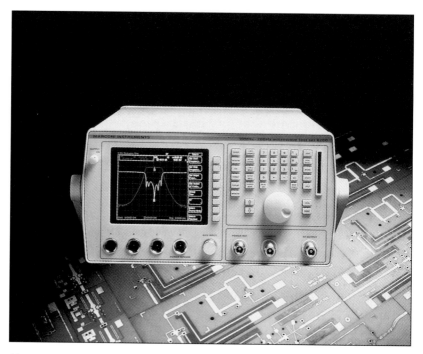

Marconi Instruments has adopted a corporate structure which mirrors that of its marketplace. Groups research their own respective market sector, formulate product responses to perceived demands and lead the ensuing development programmes. A more open culture encourages engineers and designers to meet customers and suppliers and work with their suggestions. (Marconi Instruments)

manufacturing. It also requires senior managers from each group to confer regularly.

By these means Marconi aims to ensure both effective market 'focus' and efficient overall utilization of resources. Over recent years the company has also sought to accelerate its product development procedures through the introduction of a Concurrent Engineering approach and by sharpening its ability to define market requirements accurately. One of the earliest concurrent development projects was that for the 6200 Series Microwave Test Set launched in 1991. Right at the start of the 6200 development a multidisciplinary team was brought together to be given a general briefing on the programme's aims. Even individuals not likely to be involved for several months were included in this initial exercise. An emphasis on personal accessibility and communication was therefore 'built in' to the project. Marketing and engineering staff quickly agreed product requirements and man-machine interface specifications, which immediately enabled several other disciplines to start work. Software development, for instance, was previously delayed until prototyped hardware was available. Preparation of technical support literature could also begin very early in the project.

The 6200 Series was developed in half the time that previous projects had taken and sales more than doubled the turnover of the microwave business unit. Since the launch the company has continued to refine its development procedures. Several areas have been identified as particularly important. A greater emphasis has been placed on communication skills in the company's general training programmes. Risk management has been given a higher profile in current projects. Factors with particular problem-causing potential are identified early on, contingency plans formulated and a close check made on them at monthly review meetings. In addition all engineering staff have had an introduction to marketing issues to give them a greater awareness of commercial matters.

Relations with suppliers are being remodelled to place a greater emphasis on shared responsibility for design. A key supplier of microwave components, for instance, is now asked to suggest technological solutions rather than be simply required to deliver to order. Engineering personnel are also being encouraged to gain experience of the use of the company's products in the field. As a matter of routine product development staff now visit customers for consultation and observation 'several times a year'. The phrase the company employs is 'live the measurement'.

In addition, in order to ensure these changes become firmly embedded in the company's culture and methodology, its whole approach to product development has now been embodied in a New Product Process handbook. The document sets out relevant procedures in around 20 application areas from initial product investigation through finance and team organization to test and service policies.

This was just the beginning of a change programme at Marconi Instruments which included a number of initiatives to improve time to market, such as the use of QFD and CASE (Computer-Aided Software Engineering).

Supporting the teamwork environment

The previous chapter explained how teamwork can bring about better, faster products. Successful teamwork depends very much on the cultural nature and management structure of the organization. Teams need supervision and control from management external to the team, but the key to success is to ensure not too much and not too little. In itself teamworking is just one technique, albeit one of fundamental importance, for effecting successful product design and one which needs to operate in a sympathetic environment.

Case study – Weir Pumps

One company which fosters such an environment, and has developed a management structure which supports teamwork is Weir Pumps, based in Glasgow and part of the Weir Group plc. The company supplies heavy duty pumps and associated equipment for use in areas as diverse as oil and gas exploration, water supply, marine and general industrial applications. It is therefore faced with an overall marketplace whose chief characteristics are a wide range of unrelated end users, frequent demand for bespoke products and the need to satisfy stringent performance and reliability criteria. In addition, competitive pressures are imposing increasingly tight restrictions on costs and product development timescales. The company may sometimes have as little as six months to develop and deliver pumps that will have to operate non-stop, in the most arduous environments and under guarantee for tens of thousands of hours.

To cope with these demands the company has formulated a product development methodology which recognizes the diverse nature of its marketplace whilst simultaneously exploiting and maximizing areas of technological overlap. It has done so by integrating necessarily highly specialized core design competences within an overall approach emphasizing:

■ multidisciplinary management structures;

■ involvement of engineering personnel in marketing operations;

■ centralization of technical support services;

■ and continuous improvement in the efficiency of resource utilization.

This 'lean management' approach forms part of a recovery strategy implemented in the wake of the recession of the early 1980s.

The underlying management principles of Weir Pumps include total commitment to understanding customer requirements, involvement of senior management in regular reviews of product development projects and precisely quantifying the cost implications of all relevant decisions. A key insight involves recognition that the company's various markets can be served through utilization of similar sets of skills and knowledge.

While the company maintains separate sales teams for individual market sectors its product development resources are split into only three application areas. These are: Engineered Products for bespoke projects; Standard Products for off-the-shelf items; and Electrical Machines for the limited amount of motor development the company undertakes. Support for all three is provided by a Technical Services Department. The four areas constitute the company's Technical Division and all four departmental heads report directly to the technical director. This structure militates strongly against fragmentation of technical resources and duplication of development work.

At a management level day-to-day activities can be monitored and coordinated by the technical director. In addition the concentration in a single support service of almost all generic technical expertise provides a central reference point for all project work.

At the core of any project is a team of experienced design engineers, who may have only eight to ten weeks to turn an agreed performance specification into a design capable of generating detailed manufacturing and purchasing instructions. For that reason the company maintains this element of the process as a discrete, specialist activity. The purchasing and manufacturing departments, however, are formally consulted at the concept and detail design stages in review meetings chaired by the appropriate chief engineer.

All other structures and procedures at Weir are directed towards ensuring the overall integration of business and technical objectives. The company's product development executive is a committee of senior sales and technical managers that meets quarterly under the chairmanship of the managing director to review market developments, define appropriate

The corporate culture of Weir combines lean management, tightly controlled monitoring of costs and timescales, and structures and procedures directed towards ensuring the overall integration of business and technical objectives. Resources are shared where necessary and dedicated where necessary, and the company has no formal marketing department. (Weir Pumps)

responses and monitor progress of current projects. Sales and technical operations are in any case closely involved with each other.

The company has no formal marketing department. Instead 'marketing is a joint exercise between sales and marketing staff'. All sales personnel possess engineering qualifications. Many of them have moved over from an engineering position within the company. Product specifications are normally finalized by direct consultations involving customers and both sales and engineering staff.

The company's product design and development procedures are also subject to continuous analysis and refinement by an Engineering Systems Group set up four years ago to reduce costs on a continuous basis. Projects undertaken by the Group include improving the accessibility of database information, enhancing links between internally written and proprietary software programs and rationalizing materials usage. Furthermore the company is continually setting up one-off cost reduction teams involving engineering, manufacturing, sales and financial staff to examine specific product application areas. Such teams also frequently include personnel from outside the particular application area involved in order to ensure the analysis is completely objective.

Weir Pumps manages to serve a series of sharply differentiated, specialized market niches through a product development process that is integrated, targeted and efficient. It does so in large part because it finds ways of combining a highly technically specialized core design function with multidisiciplinary support and enhancement structures and with a culture in which business and technical operations can work closely together.

Case study – Maclaren

In a very different sector from Weir, Maclaren Limited of Northampton, manufacturers of 'wheeled nursery goods' have also reaped the benefits of reforming the company's structure and processes and ensuring that changes are supported by the right cultural adjustments.

The technical demands made on prams and pushchairs in terms of stability, fire-resistance and non-toxicity are very stringent. In this sector purchasers are also influenced by fashion and lifestyle considerations, and demographic change means the overall market is declining in volume terms. Facing increasing losses at the end of the 1980s, due to extended product development timescales and ultimately failure to satisfy customer requirements, changes were clearly necessary at Maclaren. The reform of the company's product development processes aimed to ensure profitability by meeting consumer needs. Specific targets were to increase modularity across different product ranges and compress product development times by at least a factor of two.

The importance of involving senior management in product development was acknowledged and ultimate authority for it now rests with a Product Development Group whose composition reflects the importance the company places on the issue. Membership comprises the managing director Denzil Lee, who chairs the group, the marketing managers for both the UK and export sales, the manufacturing director, the technical director and the latter's deputy. The MD also formally heads the company's sales and marketing operations, so there is a direct link at the highest level between sales, marketing and product development activities. The go-ahead for any new product development project is dependent on a marketing brief outlining

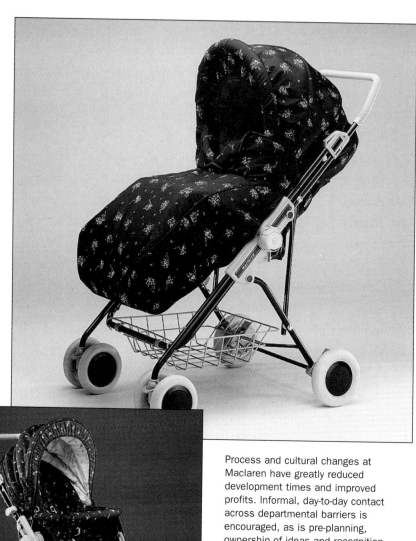

Process and cultural changes at Maclaren have greatly reduced development times and improved profits. Informal, day-to-day contact across departmental barriers is encouraged, as is pre-planning, ownership of ideas and recognition of the need to convince others in meetings. (Maclaren Ltd)

competition and perceived consumer needs, and also on an assurance from the R&D department that any technical issues have been resolved. The results of in-depth market research are fed back into the relevant processes.

A multidisciplinary approach is implemented through both formal supervisory mechanisms. The R&D department includes CAD operators, prototype modelmakers and testing staff. One individual from each category is now dedicated to any new product development project, thus ensuring that there is a multidisciplinary technical 'core' to each project to mirror the multidisciplinary supervisory structure.

Having recognized that the remodelling of formal mechanisms alone is not enough, Maclaren has made efforts to ensure there is a general culture which encourages contact between different technical and commercial specialisms. Denzil Lee describes the aim as an 'acetate culture' meaning that at meetings everyone is encouraged to make formal presentations. The value of 'pre-planning, ownership of ideas and convincing others' is emphasized. At a more general level informal, day-to-day contact across departmental boundaries is also actively encouraged.

The result of these reforms and the careful support of organizational and process changes with cultural adaptations has been a steady stream of innovative and successful products. In a 13-month period from April 1992 to May 1993, for instance, the company launched three major products: the Sherelle lie-flat, forward or rearward facing pushchair/carrycot with optional car-seat; the Chamade lie-flat pushchair/carrycot; and the Contessa lie-flat pushchair/carrycot again with a car-seat option. The products complement each other by offering a range of options across a broad price band from around £200 to £400. The company developed all three products within 11 months, whereas it took two years to develop the first version of the Super Dreamer pushchair launched in 1989.

The contrast between Maclaren's present and previous performance demonstrates the link between effective product development and commercial success. It also shows how innovation stems from the mix of a positive corporate culture with an appropriate administrative structure which combines senior management involvement and clearly defined lines of communication.

The key principles

This chapter has shown how changes in the product development process must be supported by the right culture. It is the responsibility of senior management to ensure that this happens by:

- providing training to help employees to implement changes and adopt new procedures and structures;
- encouraging accessibility and free exchange of ideas between different departments and disciplines at the same time as maintaining clear lines of communication and regular reporting and monitoring procedures;
- encouraging contact between technical and commercial specialisms and helping specialists to gain understanding of business and marketing issues outside their previous experience;
- fostering an environment which supports teamworking and Concurrent Engineering;
- encouraging involvement, ownership of ideas and commitment from the top down to the overriding goal of well-managed, competitive product development.

6 Computer support

Although many companies are now well acquainted with the benefits which IT and computer systems have to offer, many are not actually experiencing those benefits. In the UK in particular there is still a great deal of resistance amongst senior managers – often understandably – to fully integrated computerization. A considerable number of companies have also either suffered from choosing the wrong system or failing to exploit the right one, whether for organizational or technological reasons. Yet the decreasing price of systems and the increased capabilities of PCs now make it easier to justify installing a workstation for nearly every designer and in some companies every employee.

However, although computers can greatly speed up many mechanical operations, an important point to be made is that computer technology is not an end in itself and should not be seen as anything more than a tool that supports rather than itself achieves organizational and process improvements. Many of the companies which feature in this book use computers successfully but selectively and have rightly concentrated on getting process, resource, organizational and other deeply rooted problems solved before leaping into the purchase of too much new technology.

The aim of this chapter is not to examine technical aspects of computer systems' capabilities, nor to discuss the relative merits of the different systems and software available – which are in any case constantly changing. More importantly for most of today's senior managers, it explains the basic benefits of computers in supporting process and organizational improvements, and gives advice on how to avoid the common pitfalls when choosing and installing a new or improved system. The chapter focuses primarily on the benefits of CADCAM (Computer-Aided Design and Manufacturing) and EDM (Engineering Data Management) because of their increasing use and competitive value, but companies should investigate which systems and capabilities best suit their needs.

The key acronyms

CADCAM	Computer-Aided Design and Manufacturing
CADD	Computer-Aided Design and Draughting
CAE	Computer-Aided Engineering
CALS	Computer-aided Acquisition and Logistics Support
CAPP	Computer-Aided Process Planning
CASE	Computer-Aided Software Engineering
CIM	Computer-Integrated Manufacturing
CNC	Computer Numerical Control
EDI	Electronic Data Interchange
EDM	Engineering Data Management
KBE	Knowledge-Based Engineering
OSI	Open Systems Interconnection
PDM	Product Data Management
PIM	Product Information Management

In the world of computer technology acronyms reproduce faster than rabbits, but jargon should not disguise the underlying issues – and the fact that computers are only tools which cannot solve organizational or process problems on their own.

Process first, technology second

Computers are tools which can encourage and facilitate the improvements recommended in the previous chapters of this book. Putting it simply, they streamline the manipulation, management and movement of data and make it more accessible and communicable to individuals and other parties both within and outside the company. One of manufacturing industry's catchphrases is that by itself automation and computerization do not make processes more efficient – they merely speed them up. The statement is usually made with reference to the effects on shop-floor operations of high technology production equipment such as robots and computer-controlled machine tools. The point is that the processes involved must themselves be redesigned to maximize simplicity and streamlining before new technology is applied to them. This insight is just as valid when applied to the whole product development cycle rather than predominantly manufacturing operations.

Try to install new systems in a management structure already problematic and the outcome will be problematic. IT and computer systems will not solve underlying management, organizational or resource problems, which sometimes become obscured when a company installs a new system. Computerization can actually bury the causes of problems, though it is often the computer system that is blamed. This explains why there are still a surprising number of companies, particularly those that are small- to medium-sized, which remain unconvinced about what up-to-date systems can offer: their fingers have probably been burnt by previous experiences, but the problem was not necessarily the system but the situation into which it was introduced. Computers can offer immense benefits in product development, but only in the right environment.

The pace of change

Although the essential enabling capabilities provided by IT on the whole remain constant there is rarely any slow-down in the pace at which changes occur. Two factors in particular continue to ensure that the nature of the IT tools available to industry are in constant flux. The first is the extremely rapid pace of change in computing technology itself. This is manifested in the way that programs and capabilities which relatively recently were available only at great expense on large mainframe computers can now be found in the world of 'distributed' computing power represented by networks of desktop workstations and personal computers. This trend has been made possible not just by advances in hardware design but by the development of much more versatile computer operating systems which can straddle previously incompatible computer environments and between which data can now be moved more easily.

A second factor constantly driving IT development is recent changes in design and manufacturing philosophies and practices. As manufacturers have been pressurized more and more to compress product development timescales, processes have had to be streamlined and efficiency increased. In IT for design and manufacture what began with product development projects being focused around computer-generated 3D solid models has been followed by increasingly feasible transfer of design and manufacturing information between different companies in computer-readable form making it possible for leading companies to achieve globalized manufacturing more easily and to integrate their operations on a worldwide level.

Even relatively recently the preoccupation for such world-class companies has been to achieve:

■ CAD and CAM links enabling manufacturing operations to be

programmed by one set of data from the design database;

■ effective standardized means of transferring CAD data between different software programs and operating systems;

■ links between formerly mainframe-based software systems into networks of desktop workstations and PCs;

■ and justification of price levels by improved performance.

While for many small- to medium-sized companies the preoccupation is still to speed up draughting and change control with CAD, and archive and store drawings more efficiently, the leading edge of IT application in manufacturing industry has now shifted towards:

■ ensuring that integration is based on accepted OSI (Open Systems Interconnection) standards enabling users to mix and match software systems according to requirements;

■ providing software systems that can support new forms of organization and procedures, such as team-based design and development, Just-in-Time (JIT) manufacturing and improvements beyond the factory gates through customer and contractor supply chains.

The real benefits

From fast-moving fashion sectors to contrasting technology-based sectors – from Courtaulds to Rolls-Royce – CADCAM, with its advantages of computer graphics, a common database, numerical control and robotics, is a facility which has helped to bring many companies enhanced performance. In the furniture and fashion and textiles sectors, for example, even the smallest company now has the opportunity to use CADCAM systems and improve performance, provided the right procedures and resources are in place and objectives understood.

So exactly what advantages do computer systems offer? In the

Rolls-Royce Trent Engine assembly modelled on Computervision Total Product Modelling CADDS 5 System. Although large companies have usually led the way, in recent years computer-aided systems have become increasingly affordable for small companies. (Computervision Ltd)

right management framework they can enhance efficiency, quality and performance. They shorten development times, reduce rework and duplication of work, eliminate the need for visual models and increase productivity. Often much too small a percentage of a designer's time is spent designing and adding the value to a product upon which companies depend for success. Having to search for or recreate information is an inefficient use of time, and this is what the right, integrated system can improve. Duplication of work, for example updating of the same information by more than one person or department, can be avoided and changes made more simply and quickly. Computer systems can free designers to be more creative and enable other staff to concentrate on priority tasks. This leads to greater innovation and greater consistency from one design to another.

The many companies experiencing these benefits include industrial designers Hollington Associates, who find that CAD allows them to eliminate some of the time-consuming stages of product design, such as making visual models. Stoddard Sekers, one of the UK's largest carpet manufacturers, makes extensive use of CAD, not only as a valuable design tool but also for costing, ordering and interface with computer-driven sampling machines. Watkiss Automation, manufacturers of vertical paper collating and finishing systems, invested £150,000 in CAM technology. As a result, design-to-manufacture times were dramatically reduced and direct downloading of design information to new shop-floor equipment cut cycle time for sheet metal work from seven to ten days. Further time reductions were possible by transmitting design data to an external pcb supplier by modem.

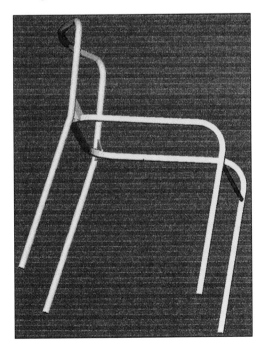

This MSc Stacking Chair was designed by Geoff Hollington and is made by SCP. Pro/Engineer software enabled Hollington Associates to design and construct the MSc chair on the CAD screen and spin a fully shaded 3D image in real time, so reducing the number of prototyping steps needed. For another client, Herman Miller, the consultancy regularly sends Pro/Engineer files by modem to the States for manufacturing. (Hollington Associates)

Teamworking and computers

Computer systems can support and encourage teamworking in the broadest sense and improve communication both internally and to outside parties. For a product development project IT can integrate not only diverse technical operations but also technical and business functions, such as the ordering of components through the extraction of bills of materials from a geometric model or checking customer feedback on existing products against new specifications. It can, as many successful companies have found already, accelerate prototype-making through processes such as stereolithography and generally ease and speed up the transition from design to manufacture as well as help companies to achieve flexible manufacturing and range diversification.

Ultimately all the procedural and organizational reforms necessary for enhanced product development and for adopting a Concurrent Engineering approach to it are aimed at facilitating the flow of information between individuals, between what were previously segregated functional departments, and between companies and their suppliers and customers: IT can improve the different relationships between suppliers, manufacturers, distributors, retailers and their clients. In fact the effective exploitation of CE relies to a great extent on the effective exploitation of Computer-Integrated Manufacturing (CIM). They cannot exist separately and should ideally be developed in parallel. Graphics, solid modelling and more recently animation and Virtual Reality make ideas and designs more visual and easier to communicate to colleagues, sub-contractors, suppliers and customers. Customers', and colleagues', ideas can be responded to and incorporated more quickly and designs adapted as required without so much rework. Not so far in the future and – in fact already happening in some sectors, particularly in Japan –

customers will be able to experiment with and order designs to their own requirements.

With a single networked database, information can be integrated, managed and controlled in pursuit of the enhanced efficiency of all the processes involved and ultimately of the quality of the end product itself. The effectiveness of communication and the ease with which information flows between – and can be manipulated by – those involved in development will determine how well they work together and therefore the performance of the final product. By being able to focus together on more easily visualized concepts and designs, teams can understand each others' ideas better.

Autohelm, introduced in Chapter 4, is a company which demonstrates the benefits of making information more accessible through a networked computer system. A small, permanent team comprising individuals from product support, customer service and the technical department provides a full-time link between the market and the company's engineering activities. Market information, which flows into the company from several sources – chiefly distributor conferences and requests for product support services from users – is collated and analysed by a further small team of marketing and technical personnel in order to provide initial development project ideas. This structure is supported by a corporate culture which ensures that all communication channels are fully utilized. All Autohelm's technical and commercial personnel can access a bulletin board on the company's internal computer network containing a list of current product-related problems. Staff can also log into the company's MRPII (Manufacturing Resource Planning) business information system, where they can see the state of orders, stocks and delivery schedules.

Knowledge-Based Engineering (KBE)

In recent years many companies have experienced first hand the benefits of CAD, and, increasingly, it is being applied to the very earliest stages of the product development process – at the conceptual stage before detail design work begins. In this context a relatively new vocabulary is making an appearance in which the crucial words are 'Knowledge-Based Engineering (KBE)', 'parametric' and 'variational' design. Each of the terms refers to a technique for marshalling more than simply geometric information, though the three are not directly comparable, since KBE is not in itself a CAD technology but is meant to act as a 'front end' for a CAD system which then effectively acts as a detailing tool. Parametric design enables product designers and engineers to manipulate geometry so that they can alter dimensions and constraints, whilst variational design, conversely, involves manipulating dimensions in order to alter geometry.

The essence of the KBE approach is that the KBE model can contain all the information needed to analyse and validate a design. It is rule-based and rules are entered using a special programming language that is a mix of normal language with other elements such as equations and look-up tables. It is impossible for designers and engineers to break any of these rules without the system signalling the fact. Designs automatically contain engineering and manufacturing requirements. Equally they can embody the specific expertise built up by individual companies in particular design fields. When designs are optimized the system will generate appropriate product geometry, which can then be passed onto a conventional CAD system for detailing or, for instance, into a Finite Element Analysis system.

Jaguar Cars

Jaguar Cars (see next page) has claimed significant benefits in terms of both productivity and design quality as a result of its pioneering use of KBE technology. Use of the KBE software system from US vendor ICAD, has, for instance, enabled the company to cut iteration times for the redesign of car bonnet inner panels from as much as eight weeks down to four hours. Jaguar became the first company in Europe to invest in the software in 1988. It subsequently set up a dedicated five-strong team of design engineers to investigate the use of the technology and began using it in real vehicle development projects in 1991. The company now claims it has gained a significant competitive edge through exploitation of KBE.

Jaguar has targeted use of the technology on development areas exhibiting several key characteristics. Crucial factors include long lead times, frequency of design, and obvious potential for optimization and enhanced consistency. The initial application areas chosen have included the design of bonnets and headlamps and the ergonomics of passenger comfort. On a bonnet design project the speed of iteration made possible by the software enabled Jaguar to generate ten unique designs. The company claims it is able to base final designs on a much more thorough investigation of all possible design options than previously and that in consequence overall design quality is enhanced by the use of the system. Use of the system for the optimization of passenger ergonomics illustrates the point. The company has built up a knowledge-based mannequin that 'knows' whether it is comfortable or not. The mannequin can be sat in the car and asked to reach for particular instruments, or its view of the whole dashboard area can be generated and assessed. Alternatively it can be made to stand outside the car and lean into

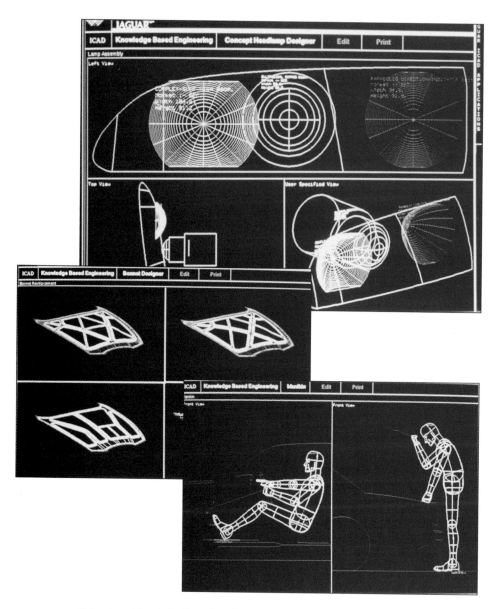

Jaguar has claimed significant benefits from Knowledge-based Engineering: headlamp design can be generated in two hours instead of three weeks; multiple design solutions for bonnets can be generated in less than a week instead of several months; and human factors mannequins can test comfortable angles and control reach. Illustrations from ICAD KBE system. (ICAD Engineering Automation Limited)

the boot in order to retrieve the spare wheel. The rules that govern the mannequin's response are essentially a set of acceptable or unacceptable angles for its limbs plus reach distances.

Parametric and Variational CAD

Parametric and variational CAD are both aimed at accelerating the speed of product development. Their origins go back four to five years, when a namesake company for the parametric approach, Parametric Technology Corporation, whose powerful CAD system, Pro/Engineer, now provides integrated solid-modelling within the CAD database, was starting up what it claimed to be a fundamentally new sort of CAD software architecture which would facilitate highly flexible design capabilities. The aim was also to provide a working environment in which design decisions have not yet been embodied in fixed geometry or where variations on existing products can meet current market demand. Originally the key concepts were:

■ a single database that allowed 'associativity' between different stages of the design and manufacturing cycle, so that a change made in, say, a 2D drawing would be reflected in the associated 3D model;

■ a feature-based modelling structure that would allow design features to have 'intelligence' attached to them: a hole would always know it was a through-hole, for instance;

■ 'parametric' design procedures that would allow users freedom to experiment within the geometric and non-geometric constraints which they set for themselves.

Since these early developments the field has become rather more crowded and now no major CAD software vendor would claim not to provide one or other or a mix of the approaches. Both

The world's first Total Product Model aircraft, the Learjet 45. Shorts, responsible for the aircraft fuselage, has used Computervision's CADDS 5 and EDM to define the product. (Computervision Ltd)

parametric and variational CAD ultimately refer to the way the CAD software solves equations to permit modifications to existing design data. This has consequences for the procedures system users need to employ to build up designs in the first place and the ease with which they can make modifications. It would be inappropriate here to go into more detail about differences between parametric and variational CAD, but what potential users need to know is that they have different advantages or disadvantages and powerful new breeds of CAD software are now available which are specifically claimed to address the requirements of rapid product development projects. A problem for many users is that both KBE and parametrics demand that the knowledge base of the whole company must be shared and vested in the CAD system – not stored in someone's head.

Engineering Data Management

At a broader level another form of software system has appeared in recent years which is highly pertinent to the requirements of enhanced product development through Concurrent Engineering. This is the comprehensive type of project management system known variously as Engineering Data Management (EDM) or, almost interchangeably, Product Data Management (PDM), though sometimes the phrase Product Information Management (PIM) may still be encountered. EDM is the term used here.

Fully comprehensive EDM systems can generally be regarded as performing three broad, related functions. These involve the management, respectively, of:

■ document and data storage;
■ product structure relationships;
■ engineering and configuration change.

The overall aim, however, is to provide a comprehensive monitoring and control system for all product information at all times in both current and previous versions across the whole organization. Relevant information will exist in numerous different formats including:

■ CAD data;
■ assembly and fit information;
■ word-processed text;
■ test results;
■ manufacturing instructions including part programs, parts lists, bills of material and production schedules;

■ commercial documentation such as requisition orders;
■ and workflow records.

In fact a full EDM system must provide a traceable recording path for every possible relevant item of data concerned with the whole product development, manufacturing and in-service lifecycle. It is this comprehensive nature of EDM systems which differentiates them from previous much more limited systems for discrete applications such as document management or the provision of management information.

Although EDM systems are being adopted by more and more companies, many manufacturing companies still do not use such systems and, of those companies that do, a considerable number still fail to manage a major percentage of product data in a consistent manner. Nevertheless, significant performance improvements have been reported by companies using EDM, most spectacularly in the acceleration of engineering change order cycles where time savings as high as 70 per cent were recorded (EDS/Design Council, 1994). This improvement seems largely attributable to the following factors:

■ better communication of development status;
■ responsive distribution of documents for review and release;
■ better tracking of 'who has done what' in the review process;
■ and removal of delays in document distribution sign-off.

Corroboration of such figures is available from elsewhere. Private research carried out by US company, Sherpa Corporation, admittedly an interested party since it is the predominant vendor of EDM software, showed following the implementation of EDM systems:

■ reductions in engineering change cycle times from 61 to 10 days with an ultimate target of two days;
■ cost per engineering change down from $4200 to $1500;

■ total new product development cycles down from 38 to 24 months with a target of 12 months (Macdonald, 1994).

If an EDM system is introduced into a well-understood development process, great improvements can be made in lead times and productivity. Changes can be processed much more quickly, data quality is improved and teamworking enhanced.

Choosing a system

As this chapter has shown, there are clearly software systems that can support organizational and process improvements. A key task facing companies is to gain an understanding of just what those systems are and how far they can help. As with any major change, a decision to purchase new technology must be grounded in a thorough understanding of company needs, resources and objectives. Whether it is first or second time round, analysis must be carried out and there must be a clear understanding of how payback on investment is to be measured and over what period.

As Stephen Gray has pointed out (Gray, 1992), companies must invest in new technology at the right level and for the right reasons. Staff at all levels must understand the functions and limitations of new technology and the appropriate management strategies must be in place. Changes in attitudes and ways of working will be necessary: the 'people factor' will kill or crown the success of a new system. The first step is to analyse requirements carefully and examine which areas most benefit from computer support. Companies must be sure also to check the compatibility of new equipment with existing internal or external systems with which it will need to be compatible.

It is advisable to shortlist suitable suppliers then set up thorough trials fully involving staff so all potential users can evaluate the different possibilities. It is important to choose a vendor who understands your company's needs and can provide support after the system is installed. Ideally an employee should learn to use the system before it is installed, but constant training and support must be provided and the system well maintained.

An appointed CAD project champion can ensure that this happens by assessing people's needs. This encourages a multidisciplinary Concurrent Engineering team approach and can help different departments to share their working environment both literally, in terms of colocation, and culturally. Allowances need to be made for the likely quantum leap in the amount of data produced and introduction must be supported by a coordinated approach throughout the organization rather than the establishment of pockets of technology of little use (Robson, 1993).

The introduction of a new system will not be an easy ride – if it is, something has probably gone wrong. The increased speed and efficiency which new systems provide can and often do bring increased demands and expectations: an analysis of resources is essential, relative to workload and skills, and training must keep pace with changes in working methods that new systems bring. Such training will at least make operation of the system less likely to be perceived as a segregated activity and not a fully integrated part of the whole product development process.

In any area in which computers are introduced ways of working often need to be reassessed: whilst some workloads will decrease others will increase and the boundaries between previously clearly delineated skills – not necessarily those directly related to using and exploiting the benefits of modern technology – may become blurred. Management must understand these sometimes quite subtle changes and support staff's changing needs and requirements.

Enlightened management will also understand that despite the many advantages of ease and speed which computers offer, there may be occasions when old methods are still valid or can be combined with computerized methods to achieve the best possible solutions. While a fully fledged Computer-Integrated Manufacture environment may be the long-term aim, the first steps must be taken carefully and there will always be some problems to be solved along the way.

Key action points

Computerization can bring great benefits but before committing to investment in new systems companies must examine their particular needs and have an understanding of the potential value of new technology to specific functions and activities. There may be underlying problems that will both affect and be affected by new systems and if these are not understood investment may be premature. When planning the introduction of new technology:

■ establish clear objectives for introducing the new system, and be clear how the implementation plan relates to your business, marketing and operation strategies;

■ establish timescales and carefully calculate resources needed;

■ examine the methods and practices that will be affected, the information channels that already exist and how the flow, accessibility, manipulation and use of information can be improved and accelerated;

■ make sure you know where the bottlenecks and barriers are and what internal or external compatibility is required;

■ make sure environment and physical location are considered: how will changes affect location of and communication between product development team members and different departments?

- involve the people who will be using the new system: give them the chance to try out alternatives and discuss with them the effect changes may have on working methods;
- provide training and support as necessary so that fear does not detract from possible benefits;
- involve your customers and suppliers in your choice and adoption of new technology;
- set up a steering committee to give strategic direction, appoint a project champion and implementation team, and ensure sufficient access to specialist advice;
- take time to choose system suppliers and/or consultants who best suit the needs and objectives of your business and who can provide sufficient support and advice in the future.

7 Making change happen

The previous chapters have shown that while there is no single, uniform way of achieving successful product development, there is a set of generic procedures and cultural conditions that collectively help companies to achieve success. By themselves these procedures and conditions do not, however, guarantee anything. Moreover, they can and must be tailored to suit individual company requirements and cultures. But if companies do adhere to appropriate operational and management principles they will certainly maximize their chances of bringing to the market on time products that can satisfy real market demands. Success achieved in any other way is only likely to be the result of luck or coincidence and is unlikely to be repeated in a sustained, structured or predictable way.

Taking the company with you

Management has to take the lead in introducing the measures that will lead to change, but what starts off as a top-down initiative must eventually become a self-reinforcing, company-wide process. A company that is consistently good at product development is one in which a wide range of staff, defined in terms of their functional departments, their team role and their levels of seniority, play an enthusiastic and proactive role in product development. Product development by old-fashioned, authoritarian methods will never foster long-term survival and will prevent employees from making full use of the skills and ideas which the company is paying for.

The evidence of the case studies cited in this book is that once appropriate change gets underway it can develop a momentum of its own. The basic necessary components for a broad-based Concurrent Engineering approach to product development – generally appropriate experience and expertise amongst employees – are latent in most companies. Some training may be necessary, but this, except when new technology is introduced, is likely to be largely concerned with communication and teamworking skills rather than with any narrowly-focused technical competences.

Understanding the implications

If problems occur – as they will in most cases – they will probably do so because of a failure by senior management to appreciate an apparent paradox. This is that though many of the reforms and restructurings necessary for the introduction of enlightened product development processes seem simple and easily comprehensible, they can often nevertheless be revolutionary in their implications for the way a company conducts itself both in the behaviour of its own personnel and its behaviour towards its customers. A company that has adopted the principles and procedures described in this book is quite simply not the same company as it was previously. It is a company that is alert and aware of everything that happens in its marketplace, not one that is taken by surprise, and one whose staff are proactive and empowered, not reactive and passive. Its senior management is visible and involved in the day-to-day activities of other personnel and not remote or dictatorial. It is a company in which internal barriers to communication are dismantled, not one in which individuals from different departments barely know each other. Above all it is a company in which corporate performance not personal or departmental status is the benchmark by which success is measured.

Measures of success

Recent research carried out at the University of Bradford (Trueman, 1993) was devoted to examining the link between corporate attitudes to product development and overall business success. It found that a better-performing company will be aware of:

■ how product development time may need to increase at the 'front end' in response to changing consumer demands;

■ the effect of global competitive forces;

■ the need to train company personnel in new technology developments;

■ and the need for detailed product specifications.

But in such companies investment in extended development time at the beginning of the new product development process is in turn offset by a corresponding encouragement of 'product integrity'. This is defined as 'a body of knowledge about the appropriateness, usability and producability of new products in order to avoid mistakes in, and speed up, the production process and ensure that products will sell'. This integrity will be enhanced, moreover, if the company:

■ uses business-to-business communication channels to acquire information on which it can base new development decisions;

88 STRATEGIES FOR WORLD-CLASS PRODUCTS

■ encourages a culture of quality, innovation and coherence in
  new products and company image;
■ constantly reviews its new product development process.

Major influences on NPD

The same study also examined what it termed 'key issues and
major influences' affecting new product development (NPD).
Analysis of survey results revealed nine such factors regarded by
companies as being of particular significance. Four 'key issue
factors' made their influence felt at project level. They were
identified as:

■ new product development process review;
■ technical accuracy and quality;
■ external and internal design influence;
■ and product performance feedback.

Five 'major influence factors' related to external influences on a
global scale:

■ company image;
■ global business environment;
■ fashion trends;
■ company and competitive issues;
■ supply and demand.

Although the relevance of these factors to the development of
successful products may be generally recognized, it is also clear
they are not universally understood. It is difficult to imagine a
verdict on new product development more at variance with the
realities of present conditions than the misplaced optimism with
which the assistant director of a process plant company was
quoted as announcing proudly that a project had taken two years
rather than one, as if that made it much more likely to succeed –
though presumably not in financial terms . . .

Keys to best practice

Research carried out for the Department of Trade and Industry (KPMG Peat Marwick Mclintock, 1991) looked at the most visible traits of good and bad corporate practice in the area of new product development. The characteristics found to be typical of the most successful companies were:

- recognition of best practice;
- encouragement of innovation;
- commitment from the top;
- tailoring and managing of the process;
- weeding out poor projects;
- devolution of responsibility;
- top to bottom integration;
- hearing the voice of the customer;
- up-front investment;
- liaison with suppliers;
- rewarding innovation;
- and recognizing the distinction between 'break-through' and incremental innovation, with an emphasis wherever possible on the latter.

The various 'recipes for disaster' cited by the research were those that might be expected. Companies themselves believed that the most crucial factors were:

- lack of market information;
- lack of skilled leaders and managers;
- poor senior management commitment;
- and poor project management.

Several other factors were pinpointed by the researchers, such as regarding product development as a 'black art' and deliberately 'leaving product design to product designers'. Both, of course, are also utterly antithetical to what are now recognized as the principles of successful product development. They imply a view of product design as an activity which is segregated, unmanageable and divorced from business objectives, when it is precisely the opposite: it should be broad-based, dependent on management involvement and existing for no other purpose than the satisfaction of defined market requirements.

The procedures that are most likely to make product development into a successful, profitable activity can be defined and designed to suit the needs of individual companies just as the resulting products themselves can be specified and developed to suit identified market needs. The case studies which follow demonstrate how change can be achieved in three companies of different sizes targeting different markets.

Case study – Crosfield Electronics

Crosfield Electronics exemplifies how comprehensive an exercise the complete remodelling of a company's product development processes may need to be, but also how such remodelling can be systematically planned and implemented. The company, based in Hemel Hempstead, generates a turnover of around £200 million per year from the manufacture of reprographic equipment, including photo-scanning and page composition systems, for use in the graphic design, printing and publishing industries. Its products incorporate mechanical, electrical, electronic and optical technologies – a complexity reflected in the fact that a quarter of its 1,600 employees are R&D personnel, most of them fully qualified engineers. Around 10 per cent of turnover is ploughed back into R&D.

By the early part of this decade the company had a well-established reputation for technical innovation; but it also recognized that it was encountering declining market prices,

Crosfield Electronics took three years to develop a new product development methodology. Consensus decisions, clear milestones and a generally more integrated approach have now improved product performance and ironed out manufacturing problems. (Crosfield Electronics)

quality problems with new products and consistent failures to meet product development timescales. The company's solution to these problems has been to define for itself and implement a comprehensive, company-wide product development, manufacture and support methodology it calls the Crosfield Product Life-Cycle Process (PLP). Development of the methodology involved three years of analysis, planning, training, reorganization, definition of procedures and phased pilot-programming.

The PLP has four essential elements. These are:

■ the Programme Approval Committee (PAC) – a group of senior managers and directors responsible for providing business and product 'vision' and overall strategic direction to ensure product development initiatives support business goals;

■ phase reviews – the procedural structure by which the PAC

makes strategic and cross-programme decisions, provides
direction for day-to-day product development work and reviews
that work at specific points in the process;

■ core teams – small multifunctional teams responsible for
leading larger Project Support Teams (PSTs) involving
everyone contributing to individual product development
programmes;

■ a structured process – a consistent, documented set of
development procedures subject to continuous improvement.

Initial responsibility for planning the process was the
responsibility of a PLP Development Team (PDT), a group of
around 10 senior functional managers. But the company does
not disguise that there were real and persistent obstacles to be
overcome. Some senior managers felt the initiative threatened
their autonomy. Many rank and file staff members were
suspicious of the apparent attempt to impose a new decision-
making apparatus. Middle management, appropriately, felt
caught in the middle. In addition the launch of the initiative
followed a separate, largely ineffective attempt to introduce
Concurrent Engineering techniques. The shortcomings of that
attempt were not, however, widely recognized and there was in
consequence a false perception that the company was
successfully implementing concurrent techniques.

Successful implementation of the new strategy therefore
required a carefully thought-out tactical approach. PDT
membership was largely confined to functional managers to
provide them with a sense of ownership of the processes to which
the core teams worked. Core team membership is kept extremely
tight and typically comprises representatives of R&D, finance,
manufacturing, marketing and service departments along with a
team leader and a facilitator, whose role is a mix of adviser and

arbitrator. PST membership is necessarily looser. Depending on circumstances, software and hardware expertise are provided by dedicated personnel, though internal resource restrictions may mean that other expertise is shared across different product development programmes. Purchasing is also a cross-programme activity.

The company supported the introduction of the process with several complementary initiatives. The first year of the programme saw a major workshop session and internal 'roadshow' involving more than 150 people within the company. The second year saw further internal promotion of the strategy including publication of a full colour wall-chart outlining all stages in the product life-cycle process from product ideas and market sector business plans to end-of-life plans and product withdrawal. Copies of the chart are now displayed all round the company's offices. In the third year pilot project teams were formed. Core team members were given day-long training sessions covering all aspects of the PLP, whilst Support Team members received half-day sessions covering the same ground in less detail. An external management consultancy was used to help the education process.

Subsequently the company published a 'Blue Book', a comprehensive two-volume document containing detailed guidance on planning and implementation issues. The document was prepared by the PDT assisted by a further ten part-time members and in consultation with around 50 identified internal 'experts' in relevant activities. The publication is essentially a repository of all product development and launch process knowledge. The document will, however, be subject to constant updating and revision. The company justifies all these activities by stating simply that: 'Defining and developing a process is relatively easy. The hard part is embedding it in the company'.

Positive results have been obtained, however, even from the very earliest pilot implementation phase of the process. These include significant enhancement of the speed and 'sticking power' of decision-making, so decisions are now consensus decisions which ensure that everyone involved has a clear set of milestones for subsequent work. PLP techniques were also grafted onto an existing development project – for the 9600R page composition system incorporating advanced 'Risc' circuitry – again with perceptible benefits. The more integrated approach led to the identification and eradication of potential manufacturing problems – in this instance concerning the drilling of holes in the densely packed printed circuit board – before production commenced. The final product also contains in-built diagnostic circuitry, as a result of a suggestion from service personnel, that would probably have been omitted for reasons of space under the previous working methods.

It is difficult to envisage a more comprehensive approach to the remodelling of product development processes than that undertaken by Crosfield. But the company's success underlines the importance it has attached to appropriate documentation and training. The company again has a verdict worth remembering: 'By itself a new framework is not enough'.

Case study – Shandon Scientific

Shandon Scientific Limited is a leading manufacturer of laboratory equipment for the specialist medical fields of histology and cytology, and employs 500 staff worldwide. Since 1989 the company, part of the Shandon division of the Life Sciences International group, has undergone a thorough reorganization, resulting in a 10 per cent increase in turnover and a 14 per cent higher return on sales. A restructuring of the company's design resources and a redefinition of product development policy have formed an integral part of the turnaround.

Shandon's basic goal is to bring more products to the market more quickly. That way it can keep ahead of the many smaller companies which produce low-cost copies of Shandon machines and can catch up with any rival that gets to the market first with an innovative product. The company has therefore set itself targets of four new product launches every year instead of previously only one, and total development times of less than 12 months.

The first step in the restructuring involved a redefinition of the company's fundamental marketing strategy as the 'automation of new or existing clinical processes'. Having identified itself as an engineering company, Shandon shed the superfluous clinical research activities. It then set about a series of reforms through which a deliberately informal company structure was oriented towards the achievement of specific performance targets.

Shandon still has a design department with 16 staff, the role of which, according to managing director Richard Atkinson, is increasingly one of facilitating communication both in and outside the company. The aim is that 'customers should specify products, the marketing and manufacturing departments determine the details of their appearance and construction, and component suppliers design the parts'. Shandon has 'broken down the walls' round its old design department. The design staff were formerly forbidden to meet customers and instructed not to consider the manufacturing implications of what they did. But now design is changing from a strictly segregated activity into a company-wide enterprise. Customer and specialist opinion is actively sought, multidisciplinary teamworking is being progressively introduced and component suppliers drawn into the design process.

The company now aims to be visited by an appropriate representative of every UK hospital, such as a senior pathologist or laboratory manager, at least once every two years. These specialists meet with management and engineering staff and their opinions are sought on general technical and business trends and the performance of particular pieces of equipment. A research department with four personnel keeps the company up to date on technological developments by liaising with universities and other research organizations. In addition, feedback from the market comes from sales personnel and a comprehensive fault-logging operation. There is a weekly meeting of engineering and customer service staff to discuss all such input.

The effectiveness of the company's reforms has already been proven with the launch of the Varistain XY, a programmable robotic slide stainer for use in laboratory diagnostic procedures.

Case study – Acco-Rexel

Acco-Rexel Limited is a particularly good example of a company's determination to eradicate departmental attitudes. In 1992 the Droitwich-based company launched a new range of five comb- and wire-binding machines for document compilation aimed at the general office market. The range was highly successful, nearly doubling the company's income in that sector after a period of twelve months. The new range was the first actually designed and developed by the company and its success was due to a new approach to product development.

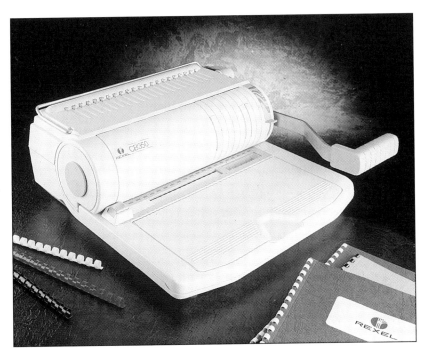

Acco-Rexel's new range of binding machines benefited from the adoption of a new development methodology, which, though the company is too small to set up formal multidisciplinary teams, involved a Concurrent Engineering approach adapted to suit its needs. (Acco-Rexel Limited)

A division of the Acco-Rexel Group, it employs 160 people in an apparently conventional departmental structure. There are five 'design' staff and three R&D personnel. Overall numbers are too small to set up formal multidisciplinary product development teams, but the company exploits its small size to implement an informal but effective Concurrent Engineering approach.

At a day-to-day level commitment to an innovative, cooperative approach to product development is evident in several ways. The barriers between different departments have literally been removed. Design staff now occupy the same office as the industrial engineering personnel responsible for programming machine tools and monitoring shop-floor activities. A new staircase has been installed specifically to facilitate communication between design and R&D personnel. These moves have taken place against a background of a general trend towards informality in the company. The fact that clocking in has been abolished underlines this.

Acco-Rexel has found that making the change to a better product development approach and fashioning a Concurrent Engineering methodology to suit its own size and structure have given it perceivable competitive advantage

Lessons to be learned

The three preceding case studies provide different examples of the problems which may threaten the design and development of world-class products and the different remedies necessary. A company may have a reputation for excellence in technical innovation but converting this into successful products in the marketplace may be threatened by weaknesses in the product development process and market pressures such as pricing. Crosfield demonstrates how reorganization can rectify this if a new structure and approach include:

■ business and product vision;
■ strategic direction of development to support business goals;
■ day-to-day direction and review of development work;
■ the setting up of small multifunctional teams to lead larger project support teams;
■ a structured approach continuously improved;
■ major training programmes;
■ visible and accessible documentation such as wall charts and a constantly updated 'bible' giving guidance on planning and implementation;

- and constant support of new structures and procedures so they are not left to work on their own.

Like Shandon a company may need to redefine its marketing strategy and the business it is in. Once this reassessment has taken place, the required adjustment and realignment can be achieved by:

- loosening up culture and communication, but tightening up objectives and performance targets;
- developing new, more positive and cooperative attitudes to customers, suppliers and specialists to ensure every kind of feedback into the product development process;
- reducing less central activities in order to concentrate resources on key aspects of the business.

As Acco-Rexel found to their benefit, even an apparently trivial change such as opening up physical access between one department and another with a new staircase, or symbolic changes such as putting an end to clocking in, can bring immediate and clearly perceptible benefits.

Each company will face different challenges and have different strengths, but whatever change is necessary, it must be led from the top and enthusiasm and cooperation inspired from the bottom up.

8 The future

Manufacturing companies depend on their products for survival. If senior management is not interested and involved in product development and committed to maintaining a culture in which best practice management can flourish and in which skills and ideas can be fully exploited in the best sense, profits will decrease and ultimately the company will disappear. The key to developing world-class products is not only adopting the approaches outlined in this book, but supporting and 'servicing' the mechanisms once they are in place – and keeping an ever-watchful eye on what is happening both within your company and outside it.

Successful companies must always be on the look-out for new trends: what does the future hold and which are the areas which are most likely to present the greatest challenges at the end of the 1990s? The increasing flexibility of manufacture combined with the immense opportunities offered by computers and IT will mean that customers will have more and more input into product design and manufacturers will increasingly be able to provide products customized according to individual end user requirements. Kitchen showrooms in which one can call up a standard design, make one's own alterations and see them implemented on screen – and even walk through a virtual reality kitchen before buying it – already exist (Nomura, J *et al*, 1994): the possibilities for designers and manufacturers are immense.

The advantages of EPOS (Electronic Point of Sale), EDI (Electronic Data Interchange), and global links between CAD and CAM so data for manufacturing can be quickly adapted and designs transmitted to a factory anywhere in the world – all these mean that companies will have to adapt incessantly to keep up. It may sometimes be advantageous to allow a competitor to blaze the technological trail before you and make the mistakes instead of you, but those who can exploit IT to meet the full gamut of customer requirements and to involve the customer more and more in the process of product development will always have the upper hand.

A key differentiating factor between companies will be the degree to which they succeed in automating design and manufacturing processes. Leading edge CAD/CAM application, as already indicated, demands fully integrated automation of previously discrete tasks. An example of this is rapid prototyping technology (RPT), which offers not only the great advantage of time-saving, but also that of allowing multiple iterations, if necessary, to optimize the final product design.

In the fields of collaboration and teamworking, IT systems will have an ever more significant influence. Design information can now be read, shared and amended electronically anywhere in the world, and multimedia technology can support the transmission of text, images, video and other data. Companies can – and world-class companies do – now choose partners for cooperative projects irrespective of their location.

Success means never standing still and change is not a race with a fixed start and finish. It is a continuous process. One of the reasons why Japanese approaches have been so successful in recent years is that eastern philosophies embody the principle of cyclical and continuous rather than linear and finite development. In an ever-changing world companies, their people and their products must forever be changing.

References and bibliography

Arthur D Little, *Corporate Competitiveness – Achieving Best Practice Planning through Managing Interfaces*, London, 1990

EDS/Design Council, *UK Product Development – A Benchmarking Survey*, Aldershot, Gower Publishing, 1994

Farish, M, *New product development – the route to improved performance*, London, Design Council, 1992

Gray, S, *The Benefits of Computer-Aided Design and Manufacture (Clothing & Textiles)*, London, Design Council (Scotland), 1992

KPMG Peat Marwick Mclintock/Department of Trade and Industry, *New Product Introduction*, London, DTI, 1991

Macdonald, D, *PDM White Paper*, Bracknell, Sherpa Corporation, 1994

Morton, C, *Becoming World Class*, London, Macmillan, 1994

Nomura, J, Enomoto N and Imamura K (Matsushita Electric Works Ltd), and Nagamachi, M (Hiroshima University), 'Virtual Space Decision Support System using Kansei Engineering', *Proceedings of IMechE International Conference on Design for Competitive Advantage*, London, IMechE, 1994

PA Consulting Group, *Manufacturing into the late 1990s*, produced for the Department of Trade and Industry, London, HMSO, 1990

Reinertsen, D G and Smith, P G, *Developing Products in Half the Time*, New York, Van Nostrand Reinhold, 1991

Robson, D, 'More Vision, Less Dazzle' in *Design* May 1993, London, Design Council

Ryan, M (Cincinnati Milacron UK Ltd), 'Survival through teamwork – the wolfpack approach,' *Proceedings of the IMechE International Conference on Design for Competitive Advantage*, London, IMechE, 1994

Trueman, M and Jobber, D, *New Product Design and Corporate Success*, Bradford, Bradford University Management Centre, 1993

INDEX

Best Practice Benchmarking

Sylvia Codling

Benchmarking is potentially the most powerful weapon in the corporate armoury. It's the technique that enabled Cummins Engine Company to slash delivery time from eight months to eight weeks, Lucas to reduce the number of shopfloor grades at one of its sites from seventeen to four and British Rail to cut cleaning time for a 660-seat train to just eight minutes. In other companies order processing time has been brought down from weeks to days, engineering drawings output doubled and inventory cut by two-thirds.

And yet, in spite of the articles, the seminars and the conferences, managers continue to ask "What is benchmarking?" and "How do we do it?" The purpose of this book is to answer those questions. Through a series of case histories and references it shares the experience and knowledge acquired by benchmarking companies across a wide range of industries. Above all, it provides a detailed step-by-step guide to the entire process, including a complete set of planning worksheets.

Case studies include: Siemens Plessey, Volkswagen, British Rail, Lucas Industries, Shell, Rover and Hewlett Packard.

Benchmarking is a flexible discipline that has become a way of life in some of the world's most successful organizations. Learning from the best can help your own company to become a world leader in those areas that are critical to its performance. In so doing you will achieve an enduring competitive edge.

1995   168 pages   0 566 07591 1

Gower

Building a Better Team
A handbook for managers and facilitators

Peter Moxon

Team leadership and team development are central to the modern manager's ability to "achieve results through other people". Successful team building requires knowledge and skill, and the aim of this handbook is to provide both. Using a unique blend of concepts, practical guidance and exercises, the author explains both the why and the how of team development.

Drawing on his extensive experience as manager and consultant, Peter Moxon describes how groups develop, how trust and openness can be encouraged, and the likely problems overcome. As well as detailed advice on the planning and running of teambuilding programmes the book contains a series of activities, each one including all necessary instructions and support material.

Irrespective of the size or type of organization involved, *Building a Better Team* offers a practical, comprehensive guide to managers, facilitators and team leaders seeking improved performance.

Contents

1993   208 pages   0 566 07424 9

Gower

Developing Corporate Competence
A High-Performance Agenda for Managing Organizations

William Tate

In most organizations there is a striking difference between what managers are capable of doing, and what managers choose to do and are allowed to do. HRD specialists often devote themselves to developing individual managerial competence with little regard to the context or the organization's side of the bargain.

In this challenging book William Tate shows how to link management development with the culture and problems of the organization to generate performance-enhancing action. Mr Tate shows how to treat the organization as a partner in the development process, integrating capability with a receptive organizational climate which encourages and applies learning. He offers both ideas and practical strategies, supported by illuminating case studies. Like his companion volume, *Developing Managerial Competence*, this engages the reader through activities, checklists and "tips", helping him or her to think through the issues and plan appropriately. He stresses throughout the benefits of a value-driven model based on openness.

This is a radical, hard-hitting but above all practical approach designed to place the organization's purpose at the heart of the management development process. It will be welcomed by HRD practitioners and senior managers alike.

1995   200 pages   0 566 07670 5

Gower

Empowering People at Work

Nancy Foy

This is a book written, says the author, "for the benefit of practical managers coping with real people in real organizations". Part I shows how the elements of empowerment work together: performance focus, teams, leadership and face-to-face communication. Part II explains how to manage the process of empowerment, even in a climate of "downsizing" and "delayering". It includes chapters on networking, listening, running effective team meetings, giving feedback, training and using employee surveys. Part III contains case studies of IBM and British Telecom and examines the way they have developed employee communication to help achieve corporate objectives.

The final section comprises a review of communication channels that can be used to enhance the empowerment process, an extensive set of survey questions to be selected on a "pick and mix" basis and an annotated guide to further reading.

Empowerment is probably the most important concept in the world of management today, and Nancy Foy's new book will go a long way towards helping managers to "make it happen".

Contents

1994   288 pages   0 566 07436 2

Gower

The Goal

Beating the Competition
Second Edition

Eliyahu M Goldratt and Jeff Cox

Written in a fast-paced thriller style, *The Goal* is the gripping novel which is transforming management thinking throughout the Western world.

Alex Rogo is a harried plant manager working ever more desperately to try to improve performance. His factory is rapidly heading for disaster. So is his marriage. He has ninety days to save his plant – or it will be closed by corporate HQ, with hundreds of job losses. It takes a chance meeting with a colleague from student days – Jonah – to help him break out of conventional ways of thinking to see what needs to be done.

The story of Alex's fight to save his plant is more than compulsive reading. It contains a serious message for all managers in industry and explains the ideas which underlie the Theory of Constraints (TOC) developed by Eli Goldratt – the author described by Fortune as 'a guru to industry' and by Businessweek as a 'genius'.

As a result of the phenomenal and continuing success of *The Goal*, there has been growing demand for a follow-up. Eliyahu Goldratt has now written ten further chapters which continues the story of Alex Rogo as he makes the transition from Plant Manager to Divisional Manager. Having achieved the turnround of his plant, Alex now attempts to apply all that Jonah has taught him, not to crisis management, but to ongoing improvement.

These new chapters reinforce the thinking process utilised in the first edition of *The Goal* and apply them to a wider management context with the aim of stimulating readers into using the technique in their own environment.

1993   352 pages   0 566 07417 6 Hardback   0 566 07418 4 Paperback

Gower

Gower Handbook of Project Management
Second Edition

Edited by Dennis Lock

The first edition of this handbook was published in 1987 under the title *Project Management Handbook*. With its uniquely authoritative and comprehensive coverage of the subject, it quickly established itself as the standard work.

For this new edition the text has been revised and updated throughout to reflect recent developments. Eight entirely new chapters have been added dealing with such diverse topics as the impact of the European Community, project investment appraisal and environmental responsibility. More than twenty individuals and organizations have pooled their knowledge and experience to produce a practical treatment which ranges from first principles to some of the most advanced techniques now in use. It is difficult to imagine anyone concerned with industrial or commercial projects who would not profit from a study of this handbook.

Summary of Contents

Part I: Project Management and its Organization • Part II: Contract Administration • Part III Accounting and Finance • Part IV: Planning and Scheduling • Part V: Managing Project Materials • Part VI: Computers in Project Management • Part VII: Managing Progress and Performance.

1994   671 pages   0 566 07391 9

Gower

Gower Handbook of Quality Management
Second Edition

Edited by Dennis Lock

Quality is one of the supreme challenges facing the industrial community worldwide. *Gower Handbook of Quality Management* captures the expertise of more than twenty experienced contributors and covers all important aspects of the subject. The text is presented in a practical, easy-to-read style and supported by numerous illustrations.

This is an extensively revised and expanded version of a successful earlier edition. Among the many new chapters are those which deal with: • benchmarking • BS 5750/ISO 9000 certification • corporate culture • customer service • inspection and testing equipment • materials handling • quality function deployment • total quality management • value engineering.

Dennis Lock has also provided a wealth of suggestions for further reading and a useful list of quality organizations.

Summary of Contents
Part 1 Quality Policy and Concepts • Part 2 Quality Related Costs and Benefits • Part 3 Legislation and Standards • Part 4 Quality Organization and Administration • Part 5 Quality in Design and Engineering • Part 6 Purchasing and Materials Handling • Part 7 Statistical Process Control • Part 8 Quality Functions in Manufacturing • Part 9 Participative Quality Improvement.

1994   832 pages   0 566 07451 6

Gower

Licensing
The International Sale of Patents and Technical Knowhow

Michael Z Brooke and John M Skilbeck

This book is designed to take the reader through the maze of activities necessary for the successful selling of technical expertise internationally. It provides a comprehensive review of licensing for the practitioner: how and where licensing is used, the kinds of business supported, the opportunities, the problems and their solutions, together with other relevant issues.

After Part 1, which summarizes current usage, Part 2 examines the strategic aspects of licensing as a method of operating outside the home country; the relevant decisions are listed as are other options such as investment and franchising.

In Part 3 the authors turn to legal and political issues and include a specimen agreement. Part 4 deals with the managerial issues – including organizing, planning, financing, marketing and staffing – and concludes by examining the vexed question of relationships between licensor and licensee.

Part 5 looks at special considerations for particular nations and regions (including the developing world) while Part 6 summarizes and looks to the future.

The result is a comprehensive and up-to-date view of the issues and questions that face the licensing executive, together with practical guidance on dealing with these issues effectively.

1994   452 pages   0 566 07461 3

Gower

Opportunity Spotting
Creativity for Corporate Growth

Nigel MacLennan

Ideas are the life blood of every organization. Whether it's the search for new products and services or the need to adapt to rapidly changing markets, the company that fails to exploit available opportunities is doomed. This unusual new book sets out a systematic approach to opportunity-seeking. It provides strategies for generating ideas and exploiting openings in a wide range of contexts.

Practising the creativity he preaches, Nigel MacLennan illustrates the text with cartoons, real-life commercial examples and exercises designed to develop the reader's own skill. In addition to describing techniques for identifying opportunities, he shows how to recognize those with the greatest potential, how to overcome the inevitable barriers, how to turn promising ideas into actual revenue – and how to achieve an organizational culture in which everyone becomes opportunity-minded.

Contents

1994   160 pages   0 566 07497 4

Gower

Problem Solving for Results

Victor Newman

In this thought-provoking book Dr Newman looks beyond the conventional techniques of problem solving to the underlying process. He identifies eight stages and explains how to recognize which technique is appropriate to which stage. On this basis managers can generate solutions at both the personal and the organizational level.

He shows
- how to overcome the four main obstacles to developing a balanced problem solving style
- how to manage the relationship between problem solving style and stress
- how to use physical movement as an aid to problem solving.

A unique feature of the book is a Problem Solving Styles Profile that enables each reader to apply the material in the text to improve their own problem solving capability.

Written in a lively and practical style and drawing on examples from a wide range of real-life problems, Dr Newman's book is certain of a warm welcome from managers, team leaders and professionals of every kind.

Contents

1995   160 pages   0 566 07566 0

Gower

The Truth About Outsourcing

Brian Rothery and Ian Robertson

Outsourcing is undoubtedly one of the most important developments of recent years in the way organizations are managed. The scale of the movement – and the range of functions involved – has grown immeasurably in recent years and is increasing at a remarkable rate. Yet confusion and misunderstanding still surround it.

This timely book charts the rise and rise of the outsourcing phenomenon in business and the public sector. The authors examine both the "why" and the "how" and describe the experience of numerous organizations which have taken the outsourcing route. They examine the advantages, the possibilities and the pitfalls. Which activities lend themselves to contracting out? Which never should be? What are the criteria for deciding? How do you select suitable subcontractors – and control them? These and many other questions are addressed with the aid of real-life case studies. The tone is practical throughout, and the book contains detailed guidance on legal and personnel aspects of the subject, including a model contract and a methodology for evaluating an outsourcing proposal.

No organization should embark on a programme of outsourcing without a careful study of this book.

Contents

1995   256 pages   0 566 07515 6

Gower